Local action, global aspirations

The role of community conservation in achieving international goals for environment and development

Dilys Roe, Brian Jones, Ivan Bond and Seema Bhatt

Natural Resource Issues Series No. 4

Copies of this report are available from:
Earthprint Limited, Orders Department, P.O. Box 119, Stevenage,
Hertfordshire, SG1 4TP, UK.
Email: orders@earthprint.co.uk   www.earthprint.com
Tel: +44 (0)1438 748111 Fax: +44 (0)1438 748844
A pdf version can be downloaded from www.iied.org

Further information is available from:
Dilys Roe, Natural Resources Group
International Institute for Environment and Development
3 Endsleigh Street, London WC1H 0DD, UK.
Tel: +44 (0)20 7388 2117 Fax: +44 (0)20 7388 2826
Email: dilys.roe@iied.org

Citation: Roe, D., Jones, B., Bond, I. and Bhatt, S. 2006. *Local action, global aspirations: The role of community conservation in achieving international goals for environment and development.* Natural Resource Issues Series No. 4. International Institute for Environment and Development. London, UK.

Series design: Eileen Higgins
Layout: Internet@TSP
Print: Oldacres, London, UK.
Cover photo: Olga Jones

ISBN-10: 1-84369-634-7
ISBN-13: 978-1-84369-634-6
ISSN: 1605-1017

Natural Resource Issue Series

If poverty is to be reduced and livelihoods improved, significant shifts in policies, institutions and markets will be required to encourage sustainable natural resource management. How to go about this is a major challenge facing governments and civil society groups. Much guidance is available for farming, forestry and fisheries, but in reality livelihoods depend upon many forms of natural capital and are not amenable to sectoral interventions. This series of reports aims to present material on key crosscutting themes of significance to many natural resource sectors, including water, soil, biodiversity, carbon and climate.

Other reports in the Natural Resource Issues Series are available from IIED on request and can be downloaded from www.iied.org:

1. Rural livelihoods and carbon management. 2000. Bass, S., Dubois, O., Moura Costa, P., Pinard, M., Tipper, R. and Wilson, C.
2. Laying the foundations for clean development: preparing the land use sector. A quick guide to the clean development mechanism. 2002. Auckland, L., Moura Costa, P., Bass, S., Huq, S., Landell-Mills, N., Tipper, R., and Carr, R.
3. Integrating global and local values: a review of biodiversity assessment. 2002. Vermeulen, S. and Koziell, I.

Contents

ii

Abbreviations

ACOFOP	Association of Forest Communities of the Petén (Guatemala)
ADMADE	Administrative Management Design for Game Management Areas (Zambia)
ATREE	Ashoka Trust for Research in Ecology and the Environment (India)
CAMPFIRE	Communal Areas Management Programme for Indigenous Resources (Zimbabwe)
CBD	Convention on Biological Diversity
CBFM	Community-based forest management
CBNRM	Community-based natural resource management
CBO	Community-based organisation
CCA	Community-conserved area
CCAD	Central American Commission for Environment and Development
CDD	Community Driven Development
CDM	Clean Development Mechanism
CFI	Community Forestry International
CIDA	Canadian International Development Agency
FONAFIFO	Fondo Nacional de Financiamiento Forestal (Costa Rica)
FORMACS	Forest Resources Management for Carbon Sequestration (Indonesia)
FPC	Forest protection committees
GEF	Global Environmental Facility
GMA	Game Management Area (Zambia)
ICDP	Integrated conservation-development projects
IIED	International Institute for Environment and Development
IPCC	Intergovernmental Panel on Climate Change
IUCN	The World Conservation Union
JFM	Joint forest management
LIFE	Living in a Finite Environment (Namibia)
LIRDP	Luangwa Integrated Rural Development Programme (became South Luangwa Area Management Unit SLAMU 01/01/1999)
MA	Millennium Ecosystem Assessment
MDG	Millennium Development Goal
MEA	Multilateral Environmental Agreement
NBSAP	The National Biodiversity Strategy and Action Plan (Iran)
NGO	Non-government organisation
NORAD	Norwegian Agency for Development Cooperation
NRMP	Natural Resource Management Programme
NTFP	Non-timber forest product
OECD	Organisation for Economic Co-operation and Development
PA	Protected area
PES	Payments for environmental services

iii

PRI	Panchayati Raj (local self-governance) Institution (India)
RDC	Rural district council (Zimbabwe)
RECOFTC	The Regional Community Forest Training Center for Asia and the Pacific
RUPFOR	Research Unit for Participatory Forestry (India)
SADC	Southern African Development Community
SAfMA	Millennium Ecosystem Assessment for Southern Africa
SICAP	The Central American Protected Areas System
SINAC	The National System of Conservation Areas (Costa Rica)
UN	United Nations
UNCCD	United Nations Convention to Combat Desertification
UNDP	United Nations Development Programme
UNEP	United Nations Environment Programme
UNFCCC	United Nations Framework Convention on Climate Change
UNRISD	United Nations Research Institute for Social Development
USAID	United States Agency for International Development
WCED	World Commission on Environment and Development
WMAC	Wildlife Management Advisory Council (Canada)
WRI	World Resources Institute
WWF	World Wide Fund for Nature (Previously known as the World Wildlife Fund)

Acknowledgments

The authors would like to thank the Norwegian Ministry of Environment for commissioning this study and in particular, Leif John Fosse for his help and guidance throughout this process. Insights on community conservation in Central America were provided by CoopeSoliDar R.L and IUCN MesoAmerica who produced a contributing document 'Advances in the Fulfilment of the Millennium Goals: The Central American Vision'. Associates who participated in this effort were: Carla Amador, Vivienne Solís Rivera, Patricia Madrigal Cordero, Guiselle Rodriguez, Jackie Siles and Marianela Cedeño. Mike Nurse at RECOFTC in Bangkok provided pointers to useful sources of information on South East Asia while Thor Larsen from Agricultural University of Norway (Noragric) provided some contrasting examples from northern hemisphere countries. Maria Berlekom from SwedBio provided a very thorough and helpful review of the first draft and James Mayers provided comments on the second. Finally, Nicole Armitage at IIED provided valuable support compiling references, editing, and generally keeping the study on track. The opinions expressed in this report are those of the authors and not necessarily those of the Norwegian Ministry of Environment.

The production of this report overlapped with another report commissioned by the Norwegian Agency for Development Cooperation (NORAD) from IIED - 'Environmental governance: *Implications for donors from the practice of governance in agriculture, forestry and urban development.*' This report concludes that there has been insufficient investment by donors in environmental assets. Further, the key issue of natural resource governance in developing countries has often been marginalised or neglected altogether. The evidence reviewed suggests that addressing the governance of natural resources is a necessary step to enhanced resource management as well as improved livelihoods for poor households who depend on natural resources.

Can community conservation bring international goals down to earth?

Assessing community conservation as a route to achieving the Millennium Development Goals and Multilateral Environmental Agreements in light of the Millennium Ecosystem Assessment

Summary

1. The Millennium Ecosystem Assessment (MA) emphasises the inter-relationship between ecosystem health and human well-being. The degradation of ecosystem services represents the loss of one of humankind's capital assets. Biodiversity underpins the delivery of these ecosystem services and hence biodiversity conservation is essential for securing human well-being.

2. One of the dramatic observations from the MA is that most of the ecosystem services were found to be disturbed to such an extent that reaching the Convention on Biological Diversity (CBD) goal of a significant reduction in the rate of loss of biodiversity by 2010, or the Millennium Development Goals (MDGs) by 2015, could prove impossible unless remedial action is taken urgently. Could community conservation be part of that remedial action?

3. The MA emphasises that: "Measures to conserve natural resources are more likely to succeed if local communities are given ownership of them, share the benefits and are involved in decisions." and that "a number of community-based resource management programs have slowed the loss of biodiversity while contributing benefits to the people..." At the same time, the MA is not blind to many of the challenges facing community conservation initiatives, recognising that capturing local benefits has been one of the more problematic responses to biodiversity loss: "While "win-win" opportunities for biodiversity conservation and local community benefits do exist, local communities can often achieve greater economic benefits from actions that lead to biodiversity loss."

4. The CBD also acknowledges the central role of communities. Various articles emphasise the importance of traditional knowledge, equitable sharing of benefits, and customary use while the 'ecosystem approach' adopted by the CBD includes the principle of decentralisation to the lowest appropriate level of management.

v

5. The MDGs make no specific provision for community conservation. In fact they make very little provision for conservation at all. MDG7 – 'Ensure Environmental Sustainability' – expressly deals with environmental issues but while the MA (and to some extent the CBD) emphasises the linkages between ecosystem services and human well-being, the MDGs separate 'environment' out into one of eight goals rather than integrating it across the goals. However, just as biodiversity underpins the provision of ecosystem services and ecosystem services contribute to human well-being within the MA conceptual framework, so the wise use of biodiversity clearly underpins the range of development priorities encompassed by all eight MDGs.

6. Community conservation can contribute to human well-being both directly – for example, through income-earning opportunities, local empowerment, and increased security of resource access – and indirectly, though biodiversity conservation and the impact this has on ecosystem services.

7. A review of community conservation – focusing mainly on southern Africa but also drawing on experience in India, South East Asia and Central America – provides clear evidence of this contribution (methodological difficulties in measuring impacts and attributing causality notwithstanding):

- Cash income – generally not that significant at the individual or household level, but can be substantial at the community level e.g. US$350,000 in 2002 for the Sankuyo community in Botswana and US$154,000 in 2003 for the Nyae Nyae community in Namibia; US$ 1,500 per village forest protection committee for JFM (joint forest management) in West Bengal in the year 2000-2001.

- Jobs – only a limited number but may often be the only formal employment opportunities available in remote rural areas.

- Enterprise opportunities – as with employment, community conservation initiatives can lead to the development of associated enterprises such as the manufacture of charcoal or the production and sale of handicrafts.

- Subsistence resources – large numbers of people in southern Africa depend on natural resources for food, fodder, medicines and building materials. The role of wild plants and animals is critical in their livelihoods especially in periods of stress. It is estimated that market value of everyday resource use to the South African economy alone is estimated to be around US$800 million per annum.

- Increased availability of water, improved soil fertility – improved agricultural productivity and natural regeneration.

- Empowerment - of communities vis-à-vis the state, and marginalised groups (e.g. women) vis-à-vis the rest of the community.

- Improvements to biodiversity status – through the maintenance of wildlife habitat and extension of conservation land; the development of corridors between existing protected areas; the recovery of depleted populations and occasionally the reintroduction of locally extinct species.

- Overall impact – healthier biodiversity, more diverse livelihood strategies and increased security and decreased vulnerability to external shocks.

8. However, community conservation is not without its costs. This review highlights both the direct and indirect costs, such as:

- Widening inequality - rural communities are not homogenous and community conservation can lead to greater division between different economic groups (the 'haves' and 'have-nots').

- Equitable allocation of resources – when benefits accrue to communities, there are often difficulties and costs associated with ensuring that over time the benefits are spread across a community.

- Opportunity cost – the opportunity cost of land is seldom zero. If land is set aside for conservation there is generally a cost of an alternative use forgone.

- Access to key resources – areas set aside for conservation may limit the access to key natural resources by some community members.

9. Do these achievements add up to improvements in ecosystem services – the essential requirement for human wellbeing? In southern Africa, formal (i.e. donor-driven, projectised) community conservation has focused largely on species conservation. This is only one of eleven responses to biodiversity loss that the MA identifies. It is an essential activity – but is insufficient unless linked to broader initiatives. Yet there is comparatively little recognition of the lower profile, often 'home-grown' initiatives that focus on fisheries, eco-agriculture, watershed conservation and so on. This is less the case in many other regions – notably India – where community conservation initiatives are typically associated with the management of forests rather than large mammals and therefore inevitably address conservation at a much wider scale. Furthermore, the project approach to community conservation prevalent across southern Africa is less common in India, where there is a greater focus on traditional institutions, community-conserved areas and so on.

10. At the local level, community conservation can help address the direct drivers of biodiversity loss and poverty. At the national and global level however, these drivers are way beyond the reach of community action – these include demographic pressure (and the implication this has for urbanisation, resource consumption, and food production); globalisation processes; economic and trade

policies and so on. Without adequate attention to these issues of course, community conservation is only ever going to be a marginal activity.

11. Community conservation cannot solve the huge and interlinked challenges the global community faces in terms of poverty reduction and biodiversity loss. Without local action, however, the international targets set within the CBD and the MDGs are likely to be at best irrelevant, and most likely unattainable. Given appropriate support, community conservation could undoubtedly achieve more than it does currently. Unleashing this potential, moving beyond the small, the isolated and the site-specific will, however, require considerable reorientation of both donor and government policy including:

a. *Integrate community conservation in wider programmes.* A broadening of the current donor-driven concepts of community conservation to recognise the many traditional practices of local communities that contribute to ecosystem management, and better integration of community efforts within the formal conservation sector and other natural resource sectors.

b. *Recognise community conservation's role in making progress on MDGs.* Recognition of the role of biodiversity conservation in general, and community conservation in particular, in achieving MDGs. Community-conserved areas – including indigenous territories, communal lands and sacred groves – should be given the necessary recognition and support to complement more 'conventional' protected areas. Effective local organisations that have managed to balance conservation and development priorities should be supported.

c. *Improve community access to conservation decision making.* National mechanisms for enabling community participation in decision making processes within the CBD (and other MEAs) are needed. Community conservation is not just about the practical involvement of communities in conservation activities, but their full and active participation in conservation planning and policy-making.

d. *Recognise the importance of adequate process and time.* There are few short-cuts available – it takes concerted effort and time to make robust changes to the organisations and institutions that manage natural resources, as well as to the way those resources themselves are managed. Donors need to think further about the most appropriate role for them in community conservation. Given the changes in aid modalities, this might mean – for development agencies – exploring how community approaches can be mainstreamed into sector-wide initiatives, or what mechanisms can best facilitate investment in local environmental assets. Getting the governance framework right will be essential to ensuring that investments in conservation really do benefit poor people.

e. *Invest in sectoral coordination.* Without sectoral coordination conservation policy is undermined by other national policies. Ministries controlling land and natural resources such as forests and fisheries are rarely involved in CBD processes, and likewise environment and natural resource ministries are often absent from debates on poverty reduction.

f. *Mainstream community conservation in conservation education.* Training institutes need to offer multi-disciplinary courses or modules that give participants a breadth of understanding about community conservation, its potential and its challenges, in order to produce skilled facilitators and administrators.

g. *Develop stronger market-linked incentives, fairly.* Successful community conservation must allow natural resource managers to derive a fair market return on their investment. This requires eliminating perverse incentives including market-distorting subsidies and other trade interventions. Payments for ecosystem services – including biodiversity, watersheds, and carbon – show significant potential in providing positive, direct incentives for conservation but require more attention (particularly to equity impacts), experimentation and support. Expanding the scope of the Kyoto Protocol to include "avoided deforestation" as a mechanism for tackling greenhouse gas emissions could be a huge step forward – but vigilance will be needed to ensure poor people are able to participate in these new markets.

ix

Local action, global aspirations

1

"Given that biodiversity underpins the provision of ecosystem services, which in turn affects human well-being, long-term sustainable achievement of the MDGs requires that biodiversity loss is controlled as part of MDG7."(MA 2005b: 15)

1. Introduction

1.1 Background to this report

The Millennium Ecosystem Assessment (MA) was the most comprehensive appraisal of the state of the world's ecosystems that has ever been undertaken. The MA involved contributions from 1,360 researchers, and is set to become as important in terms of raising awareness of the socio-economic importance of ecosystem services as the UN International Panel on Climate Change proved to be on that issue. Following four years of study (2001-2005) the assessment team concluded that there has been unprecedented change in ecosystems across the globe in the last 50 years. This change has generated improvements to billions of lives – particularly in terms of food availability and security – but this improvement has not been evenly or equitably spread across the global population and has occurred at the expense of sustainability. Approximately 60 per cent (15 out of 24) of the ecosystem services[1] evaluated were being degraded or used unsustainably:

- In a number of cases, provisioning services such as food and fuel are being used at unsustainable rates.

- Human modification of ecosystems has adversely affected regulating services such as climate and disease control.

- Waste production has exceeded the capability of ecosystems to adequately process it.

- Ecosystem modification and societal change have diminished cultural benefits.

At the individual or the global level, human well-being is maintained and supported by access to a range of different types of assets or capitals:

1. Human capital (skills, ability to work, health);
2. Natural capital (natural resources, biodiversity, the environment);
3. Financial capital (cash - or equivalent);

---

[1] See the 'Overview of the MA' (Section 3, below) for a description of the different types of ecosystem service.

4. Social capital (membership of networks and groups, relationships, norms);
5. Physical capital (transport, shelter, water and sanitation, energy, communications).

While the relationship between ecosystem services and human well-being is neither linear nor fully understood (technology and other external factors clearly having a mediating influence), the MA highlights that the degradation of ecosystem services represents the loss of natural capital and thus undermines human well-being. The MA further notes that the harmful effects of the degradation of ecosystem services are being borne disproportionately by the poor, are contributing to the growing inequities and disparities across groups of people, and are sometimes the principal factor causing poverty and social conflict (MA 2005c).

For many of the world's poor and indigenous people, ecosystem services represent the very bottom line and safety net of their everyday existence. One of the dramatic observations from the MA is that most of the ecosystem services were found to be disturbed to such an extent that reaching the Convention on Biological Diversity (CBD) goal of a significant reduction in the rate of loss of biodiversity by 2010, or the Millennium Development Goals (MDGs) by 2015, could prove impossible unless remedial action is taken urgently. More changes to the world's ecosystems have occurred in the last 50 years than in the whole of human history.

An important outcome of the MA process is the emerging recognition among environment and development agencies of the relationship between poverty, natural resource management and governance:

- World Resources 2005 highlights the links between ecosystems and poverty reduction. It suggests that "income from ecosystems can act as a fundamental stepping stone in the economic empowerment of the rural poor" (WRI 2005:3).

- UNDP's Human Development Report 2005 emphasises the importance of sustainable natural resource management for reaching the Millennium Development Goals, preventing conflict over limited natural resources, reducing the vulnerability of the poor to natural disasters, and equipping them to be able to adapt to the effects of climate change.
- UNEP's Poverty-Environment Project is based on the assumption that the MDGs will not be attained unless the concept of ecosystem services becomes integral to national poverty reduction strategies.

A recurring theme in many of these poverty-environment initiatives is the need for local-level management of land and resources. This is also in line with the adoption by the CBD of the 'ecosystem approach' which includes a principle of decentralisation to the lowest practical unit of management.

The MA also promotes local-level management, noting: "Measures to conserve natural resources are more likely to succeed if local communities are given ownership of them, share the benefits and are involved in decisions" (MA 2005a: 3). In this context it highlights that "a number of community-based resource management programs have slowed the loss of biodiversity while contributing benefits to the people..." (MA 2005b: 10). At the same time, the MA is not blind to many of the challenges facing community conservation initiatives, recognising that capturing local benefits has been one of the more problematic responses to biodiversity loss: "While win-win opportunities for biodiversity conservation and local community benefits do exist, local communities can often achieve greater economic benefits from actions that lead to biodiversity loss." (MA 2005b: 12)

Following publication of the MA, the Nordic Council of (Environment) Ministers agreed to contribute to the active use of the knowledge generated and recommendations made by the MA in relevant international fora – including in the implementation of multilateral environmental agreements (MEAs) and international development policy (specifically the MDGs). Given the significant investment that Nordic countries have made in community-based natural resource management, and the MA's ambivalence about experience to date, this report attempts to examine the extent to which this approach has indeed contributed to poverty reduction and biodiversity conservation, and the constraints it faces in delivering on these objectives.

1.2 Scope of this report

This report is the output of a study commissioned from IIED by the Norwegian Ministry of Environment. The study was conducted by means of a desk-based review drawing on existing analyses of community conservation impacts, not on new field surveys. IIED coordinated the study and synthesised the main findings, with regional specialists providing detailed inputs. The geographical scope of the study is mainly limited to southern Africa due to the degree of poverty and direct dependence of its people on natural resources for their livelihoods coupled with the region's long history of experience with community-based natural resource management. We do, however, bring in comparative experience from other regions – mainly India but with some insights also from Central America and elsewhere, where these help provide a different perspective.

The study focuses on the contribution of community conservation to poverty reduction and biodiversity conservation – the internationally-agreed MDGs and CBD providing the overarching context for this. Within the conceptual framework of the MA, biodiversity is not considered to be an ecosystem service in itself, but is recognised as underpinning the delivery of ecosystem services – hence our focus in this analysis. The MA also recognises that ecosystem degradation is a result of the interaction of many challenges – including climate change and land degradation as well as biodiversity loss. Where relevant, therefore, we also consider contributions that community conservation has made to achieving the objectives of the other two Rio Conventions on climate change and desertification – given their links to biodiversity conservation, ecosystem management, and human well-being.

It is worth noting that the MA treats ecosystem health and human well-being as two interlinked conditions – not as separate, and sometimes conflicting, objectives. Although in this report we consider separately the contribution of community actions to biodiversity conservation and to poverty reduction – in line with their separate treatment in the CBD and the MDGs – we recognise that this separation is somewhat artificial (and this sectoral thinking is an issue we will return to when we consider constraints). Most communities do not have protection or conservation of biodiversity as the main motive for engaging in community conservation – although it is often a key outcome. Instead, most community conservation efforts relate to a range of community motivations and needs, including ongoing survival and continued access to livelihood resources, cultural importance, political empowerment, and others. Conservation is a part of livelihood insurance but it is deeply rooted with other social dynamics as well. On one hand, community conservation initiatives may lead to social reforms (equity, empowerment etc.) while on the other, efforts to achieve social reform could lead to conservation of natural resources. "It is essential to understand that conservation cannot be seen in isolation from the other social, economic and political processes of the community" (Pathak et al. 2005: 73).

This report is divided into three parts. Part 1 introduces the concept of community conservation and examines its role in international processes targeting poverty reduction and biodiversity conservation. Following on from this, Section 2 describes the evolution of community conservation and the changing narratives in conservation discourse – from participation to poverty reduction. Section 3 provides an overview of the MA – highlighting its findings and recommendations on community conservation and on the links between biodiversity and poverty. Section 4 summarises the objectives of the three Rio Conventions and describes the provisions they make for community conservation, while Section 5 explores the role of conservation in achieving the MDGs.

Part 2 moves to the local level, and looks at the impacts of community conservation on biodiversity and on poverty reduction in southern Africa (Section 6) and in other regions (Section 7). Part 3 concludes the report, discussing the limitations in our current state of knowledge (Section 8) and suggesting a set of policy recommendations (Section 9) for enhancing the contribution of community conservation.

Part One:

Community conservation in international processes

2. Changing narratives in conservation: protected areas, participation and poverty

In late 19th century America, the view that wild areas should be set aside for human enjoyment and fulfilment was strongly argued by John Muir and laid the basis for the national parks system in the United States and for the pattern of conservation globally (Colchester 1994). The spread of the national park concept around the world was also associated with the premise that humans and 'wilderness' areas are not compatible and should be kept separate: "A National Park must remain a primordial wilderness to be effective. No men, not even native ones, should live inside its borders" (Grzimek cited in Adams and McShane 1992); by the 1970s this vision of protected areas had come to dominate the global conservation movement (Colchester 1994).

In Europe (and also to some extent in parts of South Asia) the concepts of 'royal game' and 'royal forests' served to benefit the propertied classes at the expense of the poor. They did not, however, completely outlaw traditional rights of use and access; rather, they laid down an additional 'layer' of special rights. Colonisation by European powers in the 18th and 19th centuries, and the accompanying spread of conservation practice, did not bring with it this respect for traditional rights (Colchester 1994). The model for wildlife conservation that was globally imposed by colonial countries was based on the American approach with local people's traditional rights of use and access classed as poaching and encroachment (Colchester 1994). This approach was bolstered in the post-colonial era by a belief in state direction of the economy; in governments as major employers; and in political ideologies favouring public ownership and control of potentially productive resources.

The rise of the community conservation counter-narrative really began in the late 1980s, during which there was a growing realisation that protected areas alone were not meeting conservation objectives. Symptoms included escalating habitat loss and direct threats of extinction, particularly for some of the more charismatic mega-fauna (2001). With the increased prominence of human rights issues on the international agenda, there was also a growing sense that people could no longer be excluded either politically or physically from conservation and the management of natural resources. In 1980, IUCN published the World Conservation Strategy, which stressed the importance of linking protected area management with the economic activities of local communities (IUCN *et al.*1980). This approach was further emphasised at the 1982 World Congress on National Parks in Bali, which called for increased support for communities through education programmes, revenue-sharing schemes, participation in the management of reserves, and the creation of appropriate development schemes near protected areas. In 1985 the World Wildlife Fund (WWF) launched its Wildlife and Human Needs Programme, consisting of some 20 projects in developing countries that attempted to combine conservation and development. Similarly, in 1986 the World Bank's Policy on Wildlands recognised that the protection of natural areas must be integrated into regional economic planning (World Bank 1986). This integration of environment, society and economy was highlighted in one of the most influential documents of the decade, the report of the World Commission on Environment and Development – *Our Common Future* (WCED 1987).

Community-based conservation was defined by Western and Wright (1994) as conservation "by, for and with the local community". This concept has since evolved into 'community conservation' defined generically by Barrow and Murphree (1999) as "a broad spectrum of new management arrangements by people who are not agents of the state, but who, by virtue of their collective location and activities are critically placed to shape the present and future status of these resources, so as to enhance the conservation of natural resources and the well-being of local people and communities". They identify three categories of community conservation that have emerged in Africa:

1. Protected area outreach. This seeks to enhance the biological integrity of parks by working to educate and benefit local communities and enhance the role of a protected area in local planning (e.g. integrated conservation and development projects).

2. Collaborative management, which seeks to create agreements (between local communities or groups of resource users and conservation authorities) for negotiated access to natural resources which are usually under some form of statutory authority.

3. Community-based natural resource management (CBNRM): i.e. the sustainable management of natural resources through returning control over, or responsible authority for, these resources to the community.

Community conservation encompasses a continuum of conservation approaches. At one end of the spectrum are the variety of measures employed by protected area managers to soften the boundaries between conservation areas and human settlement. At the other end of the continuum are programmes that seek to empower farmers, on both communal and private land, to sustainably manage land and natural resources.

Local communities across the globe have managed natural resources for thousands of years. In terms of 'formal' conservation however, southern Africa was the birthplace of this 'new' approach, with some well-known projects and programmes, e.g. the Communal Areas Management Programme for Indigenous Resources (CAMPFIRE) in Zimbabwe, and the Luangwa Integrated Rural Development Project (LIRDP) and the Administrative Management Design (ADMADE) for Game Management Areas – both in Zambia – providing both inspiration and models for a wide range of participatory wildlife management projects and initiatives that have subsequently been started around the world. It is important to note, however, that the focus of these initiatives was not solely the conservation of species and habitats. As important, if not more so, was the need for community development, local self-government, and the creation of local institutions for the management of common property resources.

Adams and Hulme (2001) propose five reasons why community conservation was initially so acceptable. These are:

1. The sustainable development agenda: many of the aspirations of the community conservation agenda also contribute to notions of sustainable development promoted in the late 1980s and early 1990s through the Brundtland Commission and the United Nations Rio Conference (World Commission on Environment and Development 1987; and UN 1992).

2. Notions of decentralisation and community: the theory and practice of community conservation evolved in parallel with ideas that central planning and top-down technocratic approaches in general were seriously flawed. Community conservation approaches, which stressed devolution of authority, provided a strong and rational alternative to central planning.

3. Changing development discourses: during the 1990s, the major development discourses were also changing. There was greater emphasis on bottom-up approaches, and the value of small initiatives over large-scale projects. These ideas served to reinforce the growing enthusiasm for the concepts of community conservation.

4. Growing importance of market forces: during the 1990s there was an increasing emphasis on the role of the market. The role of the state was to create an enabling environment rather than to use fiscal instruments to mould an economy. Community conservation – particularly in the form of hunting, tourism, and other enterprises – fitted well with notions of entrepreneurship.

5. Conservation biology: the improved understanding of the science of genetics emphasised that spatially isolated protected areas would not ensure the long-term survival of many species. This implied that formal protected areas needed softer boundaries and links with other conservation lands.

7

Community conservation approaches provided these opportunities, together with the opportunity of habitat conservation outside of the protected area networks.

Community conservation 'started' (as a formal, donor-funded project approach) in southern Africa – with an almost exclusive focus on wildlife (large mammals) and on trophy hunting as the mechanism for realising the economic benefits of wildlife conservation. However, it soon spread to other regions, and to other resources including forests, fisheries, and medicinal plants. The development of the community conservation narrative also coincided with renewed interest in the role of land and resource rights. The theoretical arguments for protected areas were provided by Hardin's classic, but flawed, description of common property as the "Tragedy of the Commons" (Hardin 1968). However, renewed interest in property regimes and the description of functional common property[2] regimes (see Ostrom 1990) provided the necessary theoretical basis from which community conservation ideas could be developed (Fabricius 2004). The outcome of this mix of market forces, decentralisation, rights and resources was that local-level governance was the dominant conservation and development paradigm of the 1990s.

The initial enthusiasm for community conservation among donors and academics began to fade by the late 1990s with a number of reviews (e.g. Hulme and Murphree 2001; Roe et al. 2000) highlighting some of the limitations and challenges faced by this approach, and others advocating for a return to more protectionist approaches to conservation – coupled with emotive titles e.g. *Requiem for Nature* (Terborgh 1999) and *Parks in Peril* (Brandon et al.1998).[3] At the same time, development discourse was moving from participation – as an element of sustainable development – to poverty reduction, in response to the international development targets published by the OECD in 1997 and repackaged in 2000 as the Millennium Development Goals (MDGs).

Social activists within the conservation movement responded to this new debate, successfully aligning issues of governance, equity, and benefit sharing with the poverty reduction agenda. The World Parks Congress of 2003 marked a pivotal turning point in the 'parks and people' debate, with unprecedented attendance by indigenous people and local community representatives producing a raft of recommendations on poverty, governance, equity, and associated concepts.[4] Community conservation moved from being an activity that had previously mainly happened outside of protected areas to an activity that embraced protected areas – with community-conserved areas being one of the new governance types recognised by IUCN.

---

[2] Subsequently it is apparent that Hardin was describing an open access tragedy, rather than a common property one (Bromley and Cernea 1989).
[3] See Hutton et al. (2005) for a detailed review of changing conservation narratives and the impacts of the 'Back to the Barriers' movement.
[4] See www.iucn.org/themes/wcpa/wpc2003

3. Overview of the MA – key findings on community conservation, biodiversity and poverty

"Biodiversity use, change and loss have improved well-being for many social groups and individuals. But people with low resilience to ecosystem changes – mainly the disadvantaged – have been the biggest losers and witnessed the biggest increase in not only monetary poverty but also relative, temporary poverty and the depth of poverty." (MA 2005b: 40)

The MA set out to assess the consequences of ecosystem change for human well-being, and to establish the scientific basis for actions needed to enhance the conservation and management of ecosystems and their contribution to meeting human needs. The focus of the MA is on 'ecosystem services' – the benefits that people obtain from ecosystems. These include: provisioning services – food, fuel, fibre; regulating services – climate, disease, water quality; cultural services – aesthetics, spirituality and identity; and supporting services – soil formation and nutrient cycling. Biodiversity, including the value derived from individual components of biodiversity – particular species, genes and so on – as well as the value derived from diversity itself, underpins the provision of these services. Biodiversity loss is thus a major constraint to human well-being.

9

A key finding highlighted by the MA is that virtually all of the Earth's ecosystems have been dramatically transformed by human actions (MA 2005b). Despite an increase in species extinction rates of over 1,000 times the background rates shown by the fossil record, millions and millions of people have benefited from this transformation of ecosystems and exploitation of natural resources. In particular, the resultant increase in food production has been a major societal benefit. However, the benefits have not been equally or equitably distributed, with poor people – especially those in rural areas of developing countries – tending to be negatively affected. The problem is one of trade-offs. Modification of ecosystems to enhance one service generally comes at a cost to other services, and these impacts affect different people in different ways. Poor people are more directly reliant on ecosystem services and on biological resources to support their day-to-day livelihoods and, with limited other resources, are more vulnerable to their degradation. Richer people tend to be less affected by the loss of ecosystem services since they are generally able to purchase substitutes or switch production strategies. Furthermore, the MA notes that "the costs and risks associated with biodiversity loss are expected to increase and fall disproportionately on the poor" (MA 2005b: 6).

Another key finding of the MA is that conservation efforts to date have succeeded in reducing the rate of biodiversity loss that would have occurred without any remedial action. Particular, protected areas have contributed to reducing the rate of biodiversity loss, but they have also contributed to poverty when rural people have been excluded from resources that they traditionally depend upon for their livelihoods. The MA notes that "better policy and institutional options are needed to promote the fair and equitable sharing of costs and benefits of protected areas at all levels" (MA 2005b: 10). These options include appropriate rights to resources, access to information, and stakeholder involvement.

What does this mean for the governance of natural resources? Is decentralisation and community management the answer? The MA is not convinced, noting that "the principle that biodiversity should be managed at the lowest appropriate level has led to decentralisation in many parts of the world, with variable results" (MA 2005b: 72). At the same time, however, the MA is also not convinced by the capabilities of institutions at higher levels: "existing national and global institutions are not well designed to deal with the management of common pool resources, a characteristic of many ecosystem services. Issues of ownership and access to resources, rights to participation in decision-making….can strongly influence the sustainability of ecosystem management and are fundamental determinants of who wins and loses from changes in ecosystems" (MA 2005c: 20). Rights are critical, but on their own, rights are not sufficient without appropriate institutional support. In other words, community conservation, unless backed by strong institutions, is doomed to failure. What are needed, recommends the MA, are strong institutions at all levels – with central government providing an appropriate enabling framework for security of tenure and management authority at the local level (MA 2005c).

The MA emphasises that 'win-win' scenarios between conservation and development are highly elusive, with conflicts rather than synergies being the far more likely outcome. In this case it is essential that trade-offs be recognised, made explicit, and then managed. In particular, trade-offs between achieving the MDG 2015 targets and the CBD 2010 target are inevitable. It notes that many strategies for addressing poverty goals are likely to accelerate biodiversity loss unless the values of biodiversity and ecosystem services are factored in. Road-building, for example, increases the access of remote communities to markets, schooling, healthcare provision and other benefits, but also opens up unspoilt areas for logging, hunting and other forms of exploitation. At the same time, given that biodiversity underpins the provision of ecosystem services that are fundamental to human well-being, long term, sustainable poverty reduction (beyond the 2015 targets of the MDGs) requires that biodiversity loss is addressed.

The way forward, suggests the MA, is for priority to be given to protecting those elements of biodiversity that are of particular importance to the well-being of poor and vulnerable people and for people to be paid to conserve those elements that generate benefits at the global level. [5] Given the acknowledged challenges in finding 'win-win' solutions to conservation and development problems, this suggests that community conservation projects and programmes will be working in increasingly difficult and demanding situations.

---

[5] Experience with payments for environmaental services is reviewed later in this study.

4. Overview of the Rio Conventions: what role for community conservation?

4

Multilateral Environmental Agreements (MEAs) are international legal instruments that are concluded between large numbers of states and have a goal of environmental protection. Three such treaties were launched at the United Nations Conference on Environment and Development in 1992 in Rio de Janeiro, Brazil – the so-called 'Rio Earth Summit'. These were the Framework Convention on Climate Change (UNFCCC), the Convention on Biological Diversity (CBD), and the United Nations Convention to Combat Desertification (UNCCD). These are often collectively referred to as the 'Rio Conventions'.

The three conventions are related: climate change affects – and is affected by – biodiversity and desertification. The more intense and far-reaching climate change is, the greater the loss of plant and animal species will be, and the more dryland and semi-arid terrain around the world will lose vegetation and deteriorate. Similarly efforts to conserve biodiversity can help both reduce the rate of desertification and help mitigate the effects of climate change. All three thus have implications for community-based resource management and conservation.

11

4.1 The Convention on Biological Diversity

The stated overall objectives of the CBD are: "The conservation of biological diversity, the sustainable use of its components and the fair and equitable sharing of the benefits arising out of the utilisation of genetic resources, including by appropriate access to genetic resources and by appropriate transfer of relevant technologies, taking into account all rights over those resources and to technologies, and by appropriate funding."

The Convention specifically recognises the potential role of local communities in biodiversity conservation through the following:

- Article 8. (j) calls on each contracting party to respect, preserve and maintain traditional knowledge, innovations and practices of indigenous and local communities and encourage the equitable sharing of benefits arising from the utilisation of such knowledge, innovations and practices.

- Article 10. (c) calls on the contracting parties to protect and encourage customary use of biological resources.

- Article 10. (d) calls on the parties to support local populations to develop and implement remedial action in degraded areas where biological diversity has been reduced.

- Article 11. recognises the importance of an incentive-based approach to conservation of biodiversity.

Furthermore, while not legally binding, the 'ecosystem approach' adopted by the CBD [Decision V/6] includes the principle of decentralisation to the lowest appropriate level of management.

The CBD also has a number of work programmes addressing thematic or cross-cutting issues which have implications for community conservation. Notable examples include:

- The Addis Ababa Principles and Guidelines on Sustainable Use of Biodiversity – which includes guidance on local empowerment as well as the equitable sharing of benefits.

- The work programme on Traditional Knowledge, Innovations and Practices - which is examining, *inter alia*, mechanisms for ensuring effective participation by indigenous and local communities in decision-making and policy-planning.

- The Programme of Work (PoW) on Protected Areas which includes a programme element on governance, participation, equity and benefit-sharing. One of the targets of this PoW is: "Full and effective participation by 2008, of indigenous and local communities, in full respect of their rights and recognition of their responsibilities, consistent with national law and applicable international obligations, and the participation of relevant stakeholders, in the management of existing, and the establishment and management of new, protected areas." Community-conserved areas will be a major focus in achieving this target.

Overall it can be seen that there are clear links between the principles and approaches of community conservation and the objectives and provisions of the CBD – both promote the sustainable use of biodiversity, benefit-sharing, community involvement, decentralisation, and an incentive-based approach to conservation.

4.2 The Convention to Combat Desertification

The objective of the UNCCD is: "To combat desertification and mitigate the effects of drought in countries experiencing serious drought and/or desertification, particularly in Africa, through effective action at all levels, supported by international cooperation and partnership arrangements, in the framework of an integrated approach which is consistent with Agenda 21, with a view to contributing to the achievement of sustainable development in affected areas."

As in the CBD, the participation and involvement of local communities is emphasised throughout the UNCCD, based on the founding principle in Article 3, (a) that: "The parties should ensure that decisions on the design and implementation of programmes to combat desertification and/or mitigate the effects of drought are taken with the participation of populations and local communities and that an enabling environment is created at higher levels to facilitate action at national and local levels." The UNCCD also recognises the importance of secure land and resource tenure, and forms of decentralisation .[6]

The UNCCD places considerable emphasis on the promotion of the sustainable use of natural resources [Article 3 (b)]; promotion of alternative livelihoods [Article 10. 4]; and capacity-building of local communities for sustainable land and resource management [Article 19]. Annex 1, the Regional Implementation Annex for Africa, suggests that national desertification action plans should include measures to delegate more management responsibility to local communities [Annex 1 Article 8. 2. (c)]; diversify rural incomes and employment opportunities [Annex 1 Article 8. 3. (a)]; ensure integrated and sustainable management of natural resources [Annex 1 Article 8.3.(b)]; improve institutional organisation through decentralisation and the assumption of responsibility by local communities and the establishment of local structures [Annex 1 Article 8.3.(c)]; and amend the institutional and regulatory framework to provide security of land tenure for local populations [Annex 1 Article 8.3.(c)].

13

4.3 The Framework Convention on Climate Change

The main objective of the UNFCCC is to stabilise greenhouse gas concentrations in the atmosphere at a level that would prevent dangerous anthropogenic interference with the climate system. Biodiversity is inextricably linked to climate change – the Millennium Ecosystem Assessment highlights climate change as one of the five major drivers of biodiversity loss. Globally, deforestation and land-use changes are estimated to account for about one fifth of the carbon dioxide emissions that contribute to climate change (IPCC 2001). Changes in climate affect biodiversity – most noticeably by altering ecosystem boundaries as a result of flooding or desertification; while efforts to mitigate climate change – such as afforestation or alternative energy sources also have biodiversity implications. The disproportionate dependence of poor people on natural resources and ecosystem services, coupled with their extreme vulnerability to natural disasters and

---

[6] The UNCCD refers to decentralisation and delegation of more 'responsibility' to local communities, but does not refer to the devolution of 'authority' to communities, a crucial element for promoting sustainable resource management (see Murphree 2000) and an important component of CBNRM in southern Africa.

environmental hazards, means that climate change is likely to hit the poor the hardest.

There are no specific provisions for community conservation within the UNFCCC. However, the UNFCCC aims to stabilise greenhouse gases as quickly as possible, so that that ecosystems can adapt naturally to climate change; food production should not be threatened; and efforts to minimise greenhouse gas emissions and climate change should be consistent with sustainable economic development. Community conservation provides opportunities for off-farm diversification – a livelihood option that is likely to grow in significance as agricultural land shrinks – as well as having the potential for contributing directly to mitigation activities through, for example, community afforestation schemes. In addition, many indigenous and local communities possess a considerable body of knowledge on climate adaptation – having had to cope with climate variability for years. Ecosystem management and restoration activities that sustain and diversify local livelihoods also increase resilience and decrease vulnerability to change.

The Clean Development Mechanism under the Kyoto Protocol does not make specific provision for community-based carbon sequestration schemes but certainly does not preclude these (a number of initiatives are reviewed later in this report). Meanwhile, ongoing discussions to expand the scope of the CDM to include "avoided deforestation" have significant potential to greatly enhance the role of community conservation.

5. The Millennium Development Goals: implications for community conservation of biodiversity

In 1996, the OECD published its report *Shaping the 21st Century*, which included a set of International Development Targets – the precursor to the MDGs – and emphasised poverty reduction, rather than sustainable development, as the overriding objective of development assistance. The MDGs (Table 1), reaffirm the poverty reduction imperative, subsuming the OECD targets and, indeed, many other development targets set by the United Nations over the last 30 years.

The MDGs make no specific provision for community conservation. Indeed, MDG7 is the only one of the eight goals to expressly deal with environmental issues, and includes indicators on protected area and forest coverage. However, the wise use of biodiversity clearly underpins the range of development priorities encompassed by all eight MDGs as Box 1 illustrates.[7] Moreover, the protected area coverage indicator for MDG7 certainly need not exclude community-conserved areas and indigenous territories. Indeed, these have significant potential to help achieve Target 9 (as we will discuss below) but are not yet included in the data sources that are used to measure progress against this indicator.

[7] See also Koziell, I. and McNeill, C. I. (2002) and Pisupati, B and Warner, E. (2003).

Table 1: The Millennium Development Goals

GOAL 1: ERADICATE EXTREME POVERTY AND HUNGER
Target 1: Halve, between 1990 and 2015, the proportion of people whose income is less than one US dollar a day Target 2: Halve, between 1990 and 2015, the proportion of people who suffer from hunger
GOAL 2: ACHIEVE UNIVERSAL PRIMARY EDUCATION
Target 3: Ensure that, by 2015, children everywhere, boys and girls alike, will be able to complete a full course of primary schooling
GOAL 3: PROMOTE GENDER EQUALITY AND EMPOWER WOMEN
Target 4: Eliminate gender disparity in primary and secondary education preferably by 2005 and to all levels of education no later than 2015
GOAL 4: REDUCE CHILD MORTALITY
Target 5: Reduce by two-thirds, between 1990 and 2015, the under-five mortality rate
GOAL 5: IMPROVE MATERNAL HEALTH
Target 6: Reduce by three-quarters, between 1990 and 2015, the maternal mortality ratio
GOAL 6: COMBAT HIV/AIDS, MALARIA AND OTHER DISEASES
Target 7: Have halted by 2015, and begun to reverse, the spread of HIV/AIDS Target 8: Have halted by 2015, and begun to reverse, the incidence of malaria and other major diseases
GOAL 7: ENSURE ENVIRONMENTAL SUSTAINABILITY
Target 9: Integrate the principles of sustainable development into country policies and programmes and reverse the loss of environmental resources Target 10: Halve, by 2015, the proportion of people without sustainable access to safe drinking water Target 11: By 2020, to have achieved a significant improvement in the lives of at least 100 million slum dwellers
GOAL 8: DEVELOP A GLOBAL PARTNERSHIP FOR DEVELOPMENT
Target 12: Develop further an open trading and financial system that is rule-based, predictable and non-discriminatory, includes a commitment to good governance, development, and poverty reduction - nationally and inter-nationally Target 13: Address the Special Needs of the Least Developed Countries Target 14: Address the Special Needs of landlocked countries and small island developing states Target 15: Deal comprehensively with the debt problems of developing countries through national and international measures in order to make debt sustainable in the long term Target 16: In cooperation with developing countries, develop and implement strategies for decent and productive work for youth Target 17: In cooperation with pharmaceutical companies, provide access to affordable, essential drugs in developing countries Target 18: In cooperation with the private sector, make available the benefits of new technologies, especially information and communications *Source: UN 2000.*

Box 1. How biodiversity contributes to achievement of the MDGs

MDG 1: ERADICATE EXTREME POVERTY AND HUNGER
Biodiversity and ecosystem services are essential to the productivity of agriculture, forests, and fisheries. The soil fertility, erosion control, and nutrient cycling provided by ecosystems enables people to derive food, water, fibres, fuel, and income and livelihoods from natural and managed landscapes. Degraded ecosystems make the poor more vulnerable to increased frequency and impact of droughts, floods, landslides, and other natural disasters.

MDGS 2 AND 3: ACHIEVE UNIVERSAL PRIMARY EDUCATION; PROMOTE GENDER EQUALITY AND EMPOWER WOMEN
When biodiversity and ecosystem services are degraded or destroyed, the burden falls disproportionately on women and girls, who are forced to travel farther and spend more time in the search for drinking water, fuel wood, and other forest products. This increased burden limits their opportunities for education, literacy, and income-generating activities.

MDGS 4, 5, 6: REDUCE CHILD MORTALITY; IMPROVE MATERNAL HEALTH; COMBAT MAJOR DISEASES
Genetic resources are the basis for modern and traditional health care treatments. Some 80 per cent of the world's people rely on traditional health care systems that use traditional medicines, mostly derived from plants found in the local environment. The global pharmaceuticals industry also depends on genetic diversity: of the 150 most frequently prescribed drugs, more than half are derived from, or patterned after, the natural world.

Also affecting maternal and child health is the increased spread of malaria, dengue fever, and other insect- and water-borne diseases linked to degraded ecosystems. Loss of biodiversity and ecosystem function can lead to economic disruption, population dislocation and urban crowding, which encourages the spread of communicable diseases such as tuberculosis, hepatitis, and HIV/AIDS.

MDG 8: DEVELOP A GLOBAL PARTNERSHIP FOR DEVELOPMENT
Maintaining biodiversity and the integrity of critical ecosystem functioning will require global partnerships – encompassing government, the private sector, and civil society in developing and industrial countries. MDG 8 embodies, among other things, the commitment of the developed countries to increase development assistance and open their markets to developing-country products – efforts that should be undertaken in ways that support rather than degrade the biological resource base on which achievement of the MDGs ultimately depends.

Source: Hazlewood, 2004.

6

Part Two:

Community conservation at the local level: impacts on biodiversity and poverty

6. Community conservation, biodiversity and poverty in southern Africa

6.1 Community conservation in southern Africa

As discussed above, southern Africa was the birthplace of formal 'projectised'[8] community conservation (referred to in the region as community-based natural resource management – CBNRM). Here it emerged primarily as a response to the moral and pragmatic problems of pursuing "fortress" conservation (i.e. through exclusionary protected areas) at a time of broad-based democratisation in the region (Fabricius and Koch 2004; Hutton *et al.* 2005). The overall focus of the CBNRM 'movement' was still conservation (predominantly targeted at large wildlife species) but linked with local economic development (Jones 2004b).

CBNRM in southern Africa is largely identified with the transfer of rights over wildlife and tourism activities from central government to lower levels of decision-making, and the accompanying focused interventions of various stakeholders to support this transfer. In most countries in the region, wildlife was brought under state ownership and control during colonial times. However, state ownership and control have not necessarily proved sufficient for conserving wildlife, and many post-colonial governments have not had the resources to adequately enforce restrictions on the use of wildlife either inside or outside of protected areas (Child 2004a).

In both Zimbabwe and Namibia, early changes in wildlife legislation during the 1960s and 1970s gave white freehold farmers limited proprietorship over wildlife on their farms and enabled them to retain the income from the use of wildlife. This led to the recovery of wildlife populations on freehold land and the development of major wildlife and tourism industries on private lands that contribute significantly to national economies (Jones and Murphree 2004). On gaining independence (Zimbabwe in 1980 and Namibia in 1990), both countries used the opportunity to extend the same rights over wildlife to rural black people living on communal land. The programme that developed in Zimbabwe, CAMPFIRE, served as a model

---

[8] As opposed to the traditional conservation activities local communities and indigenous peoples have engaged in over the millennia.

Table 2. Summary of main formal CBNRM programmes in southern Africa

Botswana	Formation of wildlife trusts	Started in 1989. Initially driven by US Aid NRMP II Project. Sources of income: both hunting and tourism contracts. It is estimated that there are now over 100 community wildlife trusts.
Mozambique	Multiple programmes	Community conservation projects tend to focus on forestry rather than wildlife due to the importance of non-timber forest products. There are, however, a number of important pilot wildlife projects including marine and terrestrail systems.
Namibia	Conservancy programme	Started in 1996. Formation of conservancies on communal land with rights over wildlife. Diverse sources of income including, hunting, tourism, and non-timber products.
South Africa	Multiple initiatives	Wildlife as a land use outside state protected areas seldom an option. Some rights being restored to communities via land restitution programme.
Zambia	ADMADE, LIRDP	ADMADE programme initiated in the mid-1980s. Revenue-sharing scheme focused mainly on Game Management Areas in the Luangwa Valley. LIRDP initiated in the Luangwa GMA in 1998 to link wildlife revenues with integrated rural development.
Zimbabwe	CAMPFIRE	Started in 1989. Rights over wildlife devolved to rural district councils. Main source of income from contracts with trophy hunters. Current economic and political uncertainty placing severe constraints on community-based organisations and locally developed institutions.

19

and an experiment from which other countries in the region could learn and develop their own country-specific programmes. Table 2 summarises these programmes. [9]

The conceptualisation of CBNRM as a mechanism for wildlife conservation has changed over time, particularly driven by the provision of large-scale donor support. In response to donor agendas of poverty reduction, CBNRM proponents adjusted their rhetoric and began to articulate more strongly what they saw as the value of CBNRM for rural development and rural democracy. Jones and Murphree (2004: 94) suggest that: "proponents of CBNRM have sometimes carelessly encouraged the notion of CBNRM poly-valency in rural communal contexts, sometimes in response to donor aspirations for comprehensive solutions to the problems of rural livelihoods and development. This has raised unrealistic expectations and disillusionment, with particularly negative results when the notion has been propounded indiscriminately at local levels".

Although the CBNRM movement in southern Africa has remained rooted institutionally in wildlife departments, there are many other community-based approaches to natural resource management in other sectors such as forestry and water. Some of these approaches cover resources that local residents depend upon on a daily basis (such as grazing, timber, and non-timber forest products) and also focus on devolving rights to new community institutions. These are discussed in more detail below (sub-section 6.2.1).

6.2 Poverty impacts

Poverty is widespread in southern Africa. About 70 per cent of the population in the Southern African Development Community (SADC) region lives below the international poverty line of US$2 per day and about 40 per cent (or 76 million people) live on less than US$1 per day (SADC 2003). About 80 per cent of the population in some states such as Mozambique and Zambia is estimated to be living in extreme poverty. In most southern African countries there are long-term and serious natural and structural challenges to overcoming poverty, either as a result of climate and soil fertility, unequal distribution of resources (for example in South Africa and Namibia), or social and economic disruption resulting from pre- and post independence conflicts (for example in Mozambique, Angola, and, to some extent, Zimbabwe). In addition there is a substantial increase in the number of vulnerable households i.e. those headed by old people and child-headed households, due to the regional HIV/AIDS pandemic (Sachs 2005). Furthermore, many countries in southern Africa are still trying to address the impacts of the inequitable distribution of land under colonial rule that often condemned black people to marginal rural areas with low agricultural potential. Overcrowding of 'homelands'

---

[9] Fuller details, including references to further information, are included in Annex 1.

or tribal reserves has led to land degradation and poverty; failure by post-independence governments to adequately address tenure issues on communal lands has exacerbated the situation.

Environmental factors are particularly important in understanding the nature of poverty in the region. Although the region exhibits considerable ecological diversity, much of southern Africa can be classified as semi-arid or 'dryland'. This term refers to areas receiving less than 600mm of rainfall annually. Rainfall is also highly seasonal so that there is a prolonged dry season during which plant production is severely curtailed and where evaporation rates are usually high (Anderson *et al.* 2004). A further characteristic of drylands is the temporal and spatial variation in rainfall which increases in the more arid regions. Thus even the highest rainfall areas in southern Africa can be subject to considerable annual variation and to periodic droughts, leading to uncertainty and risk for livelihood strategies. Diversification of livelihood strategies and of land uses therefore becomes important as a means to combat poverty in much of southern Africa.

The shifting objective of CBNRM towards poverty and rural development agendas has a number of implications for assessing its contribution to poverty reduction. Jones (2004b) shows that the indicators used to assess progress in CBNRM projects have not been aligned with indicators appropriate for assessing a contribution to poverty reduction – and to the MDGs in general. There is little or no data to show how CBNRM is contributing to the specific indicators developed for MDG goals 1-6. The contribution of CBNRM to goals 2, 4, 5 and 6 will, in any case, be very indirect and one would need to make assumptions that any general increase in household incomes or welfare is contributing to the specific targets and indicators.

21

There are also a number of problems in trying to make a more general assessment of CBNRM's contribution to poverty reduction beyond the MDG framework. Usually, income is measured at the level of the community and then extrapolations are made as to what average benefits are received by households (see Bond 2001). Such averages generally mask the distribution of income between and within households. In addition, these calculations are often based on gross benefits. This means that no management or transaction costs are incorporated. Nor are the direct and indirect costs of living with wildlife at the household level included. There have been relatively few cross-sectoral studies comparing income from wildlife with other sources such as agro-pastoralism. One such study in Zimbabwe showed that the benefit received by households from wildlife in most wards is purely supplementary, amounting to only about 10 per cent of gross income from agriculture in the same environment (Bond 2001). Importantly, these figures did rise considerably in a severe drought as agricultural incomes declined and wildlife revenue remained constant, indicating the potential that CBNRM programmes have as a direct buffer or safety net in times of stress.

From across the region there are a few examples of where significant amounts of income have been paid directly to households (see Petersen and Child 1990, and Table 3). In general, the disbursement of household dividends has been strongly resisted by local government officials who accuse the beneficiaries of wasting the money. For this reason, and also because of logistics, most communities elect not to pay household dividends (Bond 2001). Where these payments have been made, there is very limited data on the impact of such income (i.e. how it is used and the proportion of annual household cash income that it represents).

CBNRM projects provide some data on the number of jobs created but rarely tell us how many people are supported by the wages of those employed or the proportion of jobs created compared with other sectors. Furthermore, CBNRM projects are not orientated towards collecting data that is relevant for measuring other contributions to poverty reduction such as empowerment, institutional development, asset provision, or strengthening security against risks.

Empowerment has received considerable attention as an important means for combating poverty. A World Bank strategy for poverty reduction in Africa called Community Driven Development (CDD) suggests that "local empowerment is a form of poverty reduction in its own right, quite independent of its income effects" (World Bank 2000). One form of empowerment is through supporting local institutions: "Poor, marginalised communities can be mobilised to help reduce their poverty by drawing on and strengthening their social institutions. Groups with a strong collective identity – and a willingness to collaborate with outside agents to forge new solutions – can work to increase their access to health, education, and other public services, improving their living conditions and raising their incomes" (World Bank 2001:125).

Moreover, strong, accountable local institutions can be important agents for increasing the capacity of the poor to engage society's power structures and articulate their interests and aspirations.

The following sub-sections draw on available data to assess the contribution of CBNRM to combating poverty in the following areas:

- Incomes and job creation;
- Empowerment;
- Assets, security and future options;
- Diversification of livelihood activities;

We also consider some of the costs of CBNRM and how they affect rural livelihoods.

6.2.1. Incomes and jobs

In general, formal CBNRM programmes in southern Africa have not performed well at generating income at household level (Jones 2004b; Turner, S. 2004; Bond 2001). At the collective level, however, income can be substantial e.g. US$350,000 in 2002 for the Sankuyo community in Botswana (Arntzen *et al.* 2003) and US$154,000 in 2003 for the Nyae Nyae community in Namibia (Weaver and Skyer 2003). This income tends to be used for recurrent expenditure such as staff salaries, vehicles, sitting allowances for committees, and for community projects.

Conservancies in Namibia and community trusts in Botswana have tended to allow income to accumulate in the bank. Two main reasons for this have been suggested (Turner, S. 2004). One is that community managers are prudent and wish to avoid making mistakes. The other is that decisions on how to spend the income can cause controversy and dissent, and the managers can be open to allegations of fraud. Another possible reason is that revenue streams from CBNRM are still relatively new, and risk-averse rural people often prefer to bank the income because they fear that government will withdraw their rights to use and benefit from wildlife at some point in the future. This threat has indeed emerged in Botswana where the government is suggesting that community trusts should no longer receive income directly and it should go into a trust fund administered by district authorities (Arntzen 2006).

Table 3. Examples of cash 'dividends' from formal CBNRM programmes in southern Africa

Country	Year	Amount in local currency	Approx. US$ equivalent in reference year
Botswana (Sankuyo Tshwaragano Mgt. Trust) (Arntzen *et al.* 2003: Vol. II)	2003	P300 per family	75
Namibia (Torra & Nyae Nyae conservancies) (Murphy and Roe 2004)	2003	N$600 per member	73
Zambia (Lupande Game Mgt. Area) (Child 2004b)	2003	ZK5 370 per adult	5.37
Zimbabwe (Nyaminyami District) (Sibanda 2004)	1996	Z$55 (mean household cash income)	5.55

Where communities agree to pay cash 'dividends' to households or individuals the amounts are usually small (and irregular) although this varies across the region. Table 3 provides examples of some of the cash dividends that have resulted from formal CBNRM programmes in the region.

Where communities are small and there are high value wildlife resources, it is possible to generate considerable income and the impact at household level can be high. In parts of the remote north west of Botswana, for example, average household income is estimated at around US$52 a month, while the poverty line for a family of seven is US$202. CBNRM income from trophy hunting in some areas can amount to US$45 a month – 87 per cent of the average income, or 23 per cent of the poverty line (Arntzen 2003). Similarly, in Namibia, Long (2004) showed that a payout of N$630 to each member of the Torra conservancy in 2003 was sufficient to cover basic grocery costs for a household for three months. This was almost equivalent to the average amount raised annually from the sale of live goats and was equivalent to 14 per cent of the average annual income (N$4,500) for individuals in the region and 8 per cent of the average annual income of households (N$8,000). However, within the major programmes of Botswana, Namibia, Zambia and Zimbabwe, these high resource-to-human population ratios are rare (see Bond 2001). The Zambia and Zimbabwe examples in Table 3 show how small the individual or household dividends can be when large numbers of people are involved.

It is difficult to find data on job creation across the region. At the local level however, employment with a wildlife operator or a position within a conservancy

Box 2. Jobs from community conservation in southern Africa

In Namibia, CBNRM enterprises (lodges, campsites, hunting, etc.) have resulted in the creation of 547 full-time and 3,250 part-time jobs. Many conservancies also employ their own staff – for example in 2003, Nyae Nyae Conservancy employed 23 people while Torra Conservancy employed eight people. In 2003, it was estimated that the total employment from CBNRM in Botswana (community trust employees and jobs from hunting and tourism) was between 1,200 to 1,500 people. For example, the Sankuyo Tshwaragano Management Trust employed 39 local people while the company that holds the hunting leases employed 56 locals. The Ai-Ais Richtersveld Transfrontier Park in South Africa generates 16 jobs for local community members. Communities (or their committees) appear to place a high premium on job creation. In Namibia, conservancies often have high operating costs because they have large staff complements. In the Sankuyo case, Arntzen et al. (2003) point out that the hunting company only needed 30 staff but employed more to meet the tender requirements drawn up by the community.

Sources: LIFE 2004; NACSO 2004; Arntzen et al. 2003.

may be the only formal employment opportunities available and may thus be highly sought after. This suggests that strategies to distribute the benefits generated as widely as possible throughout a community or conservancy are essential. However, this needs to be balanced with the reality that increasing the distribution of the benefits will reduce the level of the individual incentive. Community-based organisation (CBO) models that generate relatively high numbers of jobs bear the risk that there are few, if any, incentives for the rest of the community.

The extent to which CBNRM programmes specifically target poor people varies – although they are often located in the poorest areas of southern Africa they are not necessarily pro-poor (Turner, S. 2004). Disadvantaged communities are often ill-equipped to capture many of the benefits such as jobs and leadership opportunities. The poorest people are most likely to be dependent upon hunting and gathering to supplement their livelihoods and to be disadvantaged by increased law enforcement: "formal CBNRM may divert benefit streams away from these people to less poor elites who are able to capture the new sort or revenues that such projects generate" (Turner, S. 2004:58). There is evidence from Botswana (Arntzen *et al.* 2003) and some limited data from Namibia (Vaughan *et al.* 2004) to suggest that the poorest people are also negatively affected by the restrictions on access to game meat that CBNRM can impose. However, some of the CBNRM activities in Namibia and Botswana support San communities, which are among the poorest groups of people in these countries.

Box 3. Nyae Nyae Conservancy, Namibia

Nyae Nyae Conservancy in Namibia for example, provided 28 per cent of the jobs in the area, and approximately 35 per cent of the cash income of the 2,000 conservancy residents who are almost all San people (Weaver and Skyer 2003). The conservancy's natural resource management and support framework also strongly enhances handicraft and tourism revenues, meaning that as much as N$1 million[10] (or more than 50%) of the cash income received by the conservancy residents in 2003 could be viewed as conservancy-related. In addition, the conservancy provides game meat from trophy hunting, supports the maintenance of village and wildlife water points, and pays for local teachers.

There is certainly evidence from around the region that benefits accrue to CBNRM committee members and their employees by virtue of their positions and often due to a lack of strong accountability to members. 'Elite capture' is an assumption often made in the CBNRM literature but rarely backed up by solid data to show that it is happening. In Namibia, for example, an analysis of data from a survey of 1,192 households in seven conservancies found that: "There is little evidence to suggest that better-educated or the asset-rich are gaining more from conservancies relative to their less-educated or poor counterparts. Thus we

---

[10] US$140,000.

conclude that conservancies, if not pro-poor, are at least not being dominated by the elite" (Bandyopadhyay *et al.* 2004: 20). This does not mean elite capture does not happen, just that the evidence is usually missing or weak.

In addition to 'formal' CBNRM, increasing attention is being given in southern Africa to the value of the natural resources that poor people routinely use for their day-to-day livelihoods and the traditional systems that govern their management. The Millennium Ecosystem Assessment for Southern Africa (SAfMA) notes that "wild plants and animals play a critical but under-reported role in food security and nutrition across Southern Africa, particularly during times of drought or food insecurity and in arid and semi-arid areas" (Biggs et al. 2004: 21). People cut poles for construction purposes, gather wild fruits to supplement their food, cut grass for thatching, gather fuelwood, and use grass for grazing. In riverine and wetland areas, fish provide an important source of protein, reeds are used for construction, and trees for making dug-out canoes. Some products are traded for other products or cash. Access to such resources provides opportunities for livelihood diversification, helps to reduce risk and vulnerability, and in extreme cases can be a safety net of last resort (Shackleton and Shackleton 2004). In some areas of South Africa, 85 per cent or more of households surveyed depended upon such resources as wild spinaches, fuelwood, wooden utensils, edible fruits, and twig or grass brooms (Shackleton and Shackleton 2004). Bushmeat and medicinal plants are also important resources to many rural people.

The cumulative value to households of such resources can be high. Analyses of non-timber forest products (NTFPs) indicate a range of gross annual direct use-values from less than US$100 per household to more than US$700 in South Africa. These direct use-values are generally significantly greater than the highest cash incomes from formal CBNRM projects and programmes (see Table 3). Overall it is estimated that the value of everyday resource use to the South African economy alone is around US$800 million per annum – although this economic contribution is rarely recognised in government policies and development strategies which do not focus sufficiently on maintaining and improving the rural natural resource base, and thus potentially undermine the long-term sustainability of this valuable asset (Shackleton and Shackleton 2004).

Functioning indigenous resource management systems are essential for providing an enabling framework for the harvesting of the everyday resources upon which poor people depend: "Perhaps the most important contribution that these landscape-wide resource management systems make to alleviating poverty – or at least to providing a safety net for the very poor – is that they help sustain communal resource tenure" (Turner, S. 2004: 58). This is important for ensuring that the poor are able to maintain access to land and natural resources. Turner also argues that the "renovation and reinforcement of such systems could significantly increase the economic output of natural resource-based production, with corresponding benefits for rural livelihoods" (Turner, S. 2004: 52).

6.2.2 Empowerment

Many commentators argue that community empowerment is one of the greatest impacts of community conservation (e.g. see WRI 2005) – far exceeding any economic or environmental benefits.[11] In the Luangwa Valley in Zambia, for example, Child (2004b) suggests that possibly more important than tangible benefits are the organisational capacity and empowerment effects created by the process of revenue distribution – which involves regular elections, bank accounts, audits, and a high level of participation in decision-making by villagers.

Formal CBNRM programmes in southern Africa have contributed to empowerment of local communities in different ways. These include strengthened social and political organisations that can represent community interests vis-à-vis government, agencies, donors, and other local-level institutions. In Namibia, WRI (2005) notes that: "The process of managing a new democratic institution [i.e. the new community conservancies] has empowered those taking part and given them new skills" (WRI 2005: 118). In Zimbabwe, Taylor (2006) reports that village- and ward-level wildlife committees provide for a high level of community participation and decision-making with a transparent flow of information relating to key issues, planning and projects. Despite the political and economic problems faced by Zimbabwe, Child *et al.* (2003) found that some of these committees had shown considerable resilience and were still functioning where income from wildlife was still being received. New developments include the establishment of community trusts and cooperatives at sub-district level.

Empowerment of the poor, through "information provision, participation and power to redress" is highlighted by WRI as one of the key mechanisms for bringing pro-poor governance to the management of ecosystems. However, empowerment effects can often be transitory and are difficult to measure. Mapedza and Bond

---

Box 4. The Makuleke Land Claim, South Africa

In South Africa, where the Makuleke community successfully claimed back land inside the Kruger National Park under post-apartheid land restitution laws, a key consideration was not only improved economic conditions from access to tourism, but regaining title to their ancestral land, which was viewed as 'an immense symbolic achievement' (Turner R. 2004). Furthermore, the nature of the agreement with the park authorities over management of the restored land empowers the Makuleke to take key commercial decisions and limits the authority of officials. This example illustrates the importance of the linkages between cultural identity and natural resources management – an issue raised by the MA as a key success factor in biodiversity conservation.

---

[11] See for example the various regional reviews prepared under IIED's Evaluating Eden initiative http://www.iied.org/pubs/search.php?s=EDEN

(submitted) show an example from Zimbabwe where local power gained through CAMPFIRE was quickly eroded once support agencies withdrew. WRI also notes that "both the power and benefits associated with community management tend to be directed toward higher income classes unless specific accommodations are made" (WRI 2005: 90). These include accounting for the costs – as well as the benefits – of CBNRM; assuring equity in benefit-sharing; and acknowledging the limits to participation – particularly for the poorest or most marginalised groups.

6.2.3 Assets, security and future options

Landscapes that are being managed by communities under CBNRM programmes provide local communities with assets that increase security against risks and shocks and ensure options for the future. NTFPs provide an important safety net for the poor – preventing them from slipping further into poverty (Angelsen and Wunder 2003; Campbell *et al.* 2002), although forest products are unlikely to actually lift significant numbers of people out of poverty (Campbell *et al.* 2002). A shift from unsustainable land management practices to conservation of natural resources that provide safety nets for the poor and have important economic impacts on livelihoods, is in itself a contribution to combating poverty. Moreover, an expanding natural resource base combined with improved community rights (such as is the case in north west Namibia) can provide a range of additional economic opportunities, which may in turn bring jobs and spin-off enterprises. Financial rewards from CBNRM in southern Africa have also provided community assets in the form of local infrastructure such as grinding mills and classrooms, clinics and wells (for example, in Zimbabwe, Zambia, Mozambique) and local credit or loan schemes (Botswana, Namibia).

6.2.4 Diversification of livelihood activities

Diversification of livelihood activities is important in the marginal areas where many CBNRM activities are located. For example in Botswana, most CBNRM projects operate in remote parts of the north and west of the country where the agricultural potential is marginal, few people are engaged in crop or livestock production, and other economic opportunities are extremely limited (Arntzen *et al.* 2003). In these areas, CBNRM can bring new job opportunities in the tourism, wildlife and other natural resources-based industries. In Mozambique for example, the Associação Communitária de Mucombedzi is a community association that is licensed to manage 29,000ha of forest of which 17,000ha are to produce charcoal and the rest is for agriculture and wildlife. Charcoal-making and agriculture are the only employment opportunities available, and the association is looking to establish additional enterprises such as beekeeping, bamboo harvesting and so on (Biggs *et al.* 2004).

Box 5. Livelihood diversification in Namibia

In Namibia, Murphy and Roe (2004) found that the cash from craft sales and working in the tourism industry increased livelihood security. They also found that CBNRM enabled a number of spin-off enterprises to develop. These include laundry outsourcing to local people by lodges, purchase of thatching grass, purchase of cattle and goats by a lodge, sales of semi-precious stones, and tyre repair businesses. In the Caprivi in Namibia, craft sales between 1999 and 2001 amounted to more than N\$333,000 (approx. US\$41,000) and most of this income went to poor women. They suggest that craft sales are an example of successes brought about by the enabling environment for local entrepreneurship fostered by CBNRM.

Involvement in CBNRM has also helped to develop the skills base of community members in some cases. In Zimbabwe and Namibia, for example, wildlife committee members and conservancy members have been trained in natural resource management, tourism, and business management. These new skills and experiences have provided important assets to help individuals secure better-paid, more secure jobs (Murphy and Roe 2004).

29

6.2.5 Costs

As noted above, any assessment of CBNRM must also factor in costs – rather than simply focussing on gross benefits, which may be highly misleading. A number of costs of CBNRM in southern Africa that impact on livelihoods are identified in the literature (Jones and Murphree 2004; Magome and Fabricius 2004; Murphy and Roe 2004; Turner, S. 2004). Where communities set aside land for wildlife and tourism, households lose access to grazing, water, and other resources. This can happen on a large scale where large areas of land are zoned for wildlife, or on a smaller scale where people no longer have access to land used for a community-run camp site for example. Often it is the poorest individuals and households – who have limited alternative resources – that suffer the most from this loss of access, however temporary (WRI 2005).

'Successful' CBNRM (in terms of its impacts on biodiversity conservation) can also bring its own problems – particularly in the form of problem animals. Crop and stock losses to wild animals can have significant impacts on poor people. The loss of one or two head of cattle to someone who owns only four or five head will have a far greater impact than someone losing one or two head from a herd of fifty or more. The high increase in the numbers of wild ungulates in north west Namibia has increased competition between wildlife and livestock for grazing, browse and water (Weaver and Skyer 2003). Elsewhere in Namibia, in the eastern Caprivi region, there are serious human-wildlife conflicts developing as a result of both increasing elephant populations and a greater level of tolerance by local people to wildlife in general.

CBNRM can also bring conflict over issues such as income distribution and deciding who should benefit. In Namibia, the 'hard' boundaries created by defining conservancy limits, drawing up formal, written land-use plans, and the zoning and fencing of core wildlife areas has led to the renewal of existing inter- and intra-community conflicts over access to land and resources. There are many transaction costs for individuals called to attend the meetings and workshops convened by donors, NGOs and government, and for those community leaders involved in the management of CBNRM institutions and activities.

The impacts of these costs need to be weighed against the benefits from CBNRM that local people themselves perceive they are gaining. Jones (2001) and Turner, S. (2004) have highlighted the extent to which "economic instrumentalism" does not always dominate motives for engaging in formal CBNRM. Jones shows how intrinsic values based on an aesthetic appreciation of wildlife and cultural norms initially helped to drive the development of CBNRM in north west Namibia. Turner suggests that communities place the potential economic benefits from formal CBNRM in a broader value system that sees a wider range of livelihood benefits accruing from care for the environment. He argues that formal CBNRM approaches need to pay more attention to this broader livelihood agenda of rural Africans.

6.3. Biodiversity impacts – species, habitats, ecosystems

The Millennium Ecosystem Assessment for Southern Africa (SAfMA) highlights the region's rich biodiversity and that it is relatively intact (Biggs *et al.* 2004). At the same time, SAfMA notes that the region's biodiversity remains vulnerable to land-use change. Protected area coverage is a traditional measure of biodiversity status (and indeed is one of the key indicators for MDG7)[12] but, although currently quite high across the region as a whole (14 per cent of land area), it is unlikely to expand much further due to conflicting land uses (Biggs *et al.* 2004). In the seven largest southern African[13] countries there is an inverse, albeit coarse, relationship between the 'biodiversity ranking' and the proportion of the country that is protected (Cumming 2004). For example South Africa, which has the highest biodiversity ranking, has only 5.5 per cent of the country set aside in protected areas. Conversely in Botswana, which has a significantly lower biodiversity ranking, 17.3 per cent of the country is set aside in protected areas. This implies that community efforts outside of the protected areas are critical to conserve the majority of the region's biodiversity.

---

[12] Although see Roe (2003) for an analysis of the limitations of this indicator.
[13] Botswana, Malawi, Mozambique, Namibia, South Africa, Zambia and Zimbabwe (Cumming 2004).

Suggestions that community approaches were not fulfilling their expected conservation or biodiversity objectives were first raised in 1995 (Barret and Arcese 1995). However, the measurement and quantification of conservation success is, methodologically, fraught with difficulty. Accurate biodiversity assessments are expensive, and skilled activities are often beyond the budgets and skills of those organisations involved in community initiatives (Saterson *et al.* 1998). Furthermore, depending on what is measured, they can be misleading. Elephant numbers, for example, are often used as an indicator of 'success' in many southern African programmes, yet high elephant populations can have a negative impact on biodiversity (see Cumming and Lynam 1997).

As with the analysis of impacts on poverty, much of the impact of CBNRM on biodiversity is often assumed, site-specific and anecdotal, and it is "extremely dangerous to extrapolate from one experience to another" (Magome and Fabricius 2004). For the purposes of this review, biodiversity impacts are classified into three categories: maintenance of habitats and ecosystems; recovery of previously depleted resources; and re-introduction of locally extinct species. Examples of each are given below:

a. Maintenance of habitats and ecosystems: in Namibia, 18 of the registered conservancies occur immediately adjacent to, or in key corridors between, national parks or game reserves. These 18 conservancies provide 55,192 km² of land being used for conservation objectives in addition to the existing protected area network of 114,080 km². This is a 48 per cent increase in Namibia's conservation area (LIFE 2004). Crucially, in some areas communal conservancies do not just add to the total land under wildlife management, but link previously discrete protected areas.

    Following Independence (1980) in Zimbabwe, many of the communal lands with areas of unsettled wildlife habitat have experienced very high levels of in-migration from other parts of the country. For example, rates of settlement in the middle and lower Zambezi Valley communal lands were increasing at between 5 and 8 per cent per annum with the result that settlement and cultivation substantially exceeded the area of arable soils (Cumming and Lynam 1997). Despite these rates of migration, 12 rural district councils (RDCs) have managed to maintain wildlife habitat. Within these RDCs the areas of wildlife habitat range from 500 km² to over 5,000 km², with an average size of 3,300 km². In three of the twelve districts the area of wild land was in excess of 90 per cent of the district area (Taylor 2006). In those districts where there was a defined wilderness area these have generally been respected, see (Mapedza and Bond submitted). Conversely, in those RDCs where there wasn't a defined wilderness area, settlement has continued – albeit at a reduced rate (Dunham *et al.* 2003).

In Botswana, wildlife-based community conservation encourages the broader conservation of wildlife habitat and has the potential to maintain or preserve the open grassy savannas of the Kalahari system. This is in contrast to livestock-dominated savannas, which have been transformed into thick bush (Arntzen 2003).

b. Recovery of previously depleted resources: in Namibia, the CBNRM programme is contributing to the recovery of wildlife populations across large parts of northern Namibia, in particular the arid north west. Large mammals found in this region include black rhino, elephant, lion, leopard, cheetah, giraffe, gemsbok, kudu, springbok and Hartmann's mountain zebra, an endemic sub-species. The general trend for all these species over the past 15 years or more has been upwards (NACSO 2004). Elephant numbers have increased from around 300 in the early 1990s to around 800 at present. There is general consensus that without community commitment to conservation, species such as the black rhino would not survive and be increasing (Durbin et al. 1997).

Background levels of illegal hunting have been, and continue to remain, high in many parts of Botswana. However, in those community trust areas where communities or safari operators manage the hunting, the levels of illegal hunting are said to be falling (Arntzen et al. 2003).

c. Re-introduction of locally extinct species: between 1999 and 2003, approximately 3,000 head of mixed plains game species have been re-introduced in six communal land conservancies in Namibia. Generally, the restocking or re-introduction of species has not been used in other countries because of the costs of capture, relocation, and the management of the released species.

These examples broadly suggest that the wildlife-based CBNRM programmes in Botswana, Namibia and Zimbabwe can all claim to have had some positive conservation impacts. However, it is more difficult and premature to draw precise conclusions about the contribution of these programmes to ecological processes and potential impacts on diversity of species. The absence of quantitative data on the quantity, quality, and biodiversity value of the habitats under management is a major constraint to establishing strong positive causal relationships between CBNRM programmes and conservation of biodiversity.[14]

---

[14] Ferraro and Pattanayak (2006) extend this point, arguing that conservation biologists have failed to systematically evaluate the impact of conservation investments. They propose that only when systematic quantitative evaluations of conservation are undertaken will the real impact of investment be understood.

The scale and diversity of southern Africa CBNRM programmes is an important context for this discussion. For example, under CAMPFIRE there are 12 major wildlife-producing districts (with over 100 wards) that have benefited from wildlife on the basis of being a 'producer community'. Similarly, the conservancy programme in Namibia represents over 44 communities covering more than 10,500,000 ha of land in habitats ranging from desert to broad-leafed woodland and floodplains. The context, challenges, resource allocations and dynamics of each community are unique. Essentially, every community represents a 'pilot process'. With this level of diversity and process, anecdotal and site-specific information on both the conservation successes and failures is always possible. Quantified programme-level information on the conservation impacts is, however, extremely challenging and expensive to produce. Even the measurement of habitat using remote sensing techniques has been shown to have high error levels unless accompanied by extensive ground-truthing (Dunham *et al.* 2003).

6.4 Links to the other MEAs

6.4.1 Desertification

The contribution of CBNRM to the conservation of wildlife habitat is closely linked with the overall objectives of the UNCCD. The UNCCD has two primary objectives, which are to reduce rates of desertification and to reduce the impact of drought. To achieve these objectives, the UNCCD acknowledges the central role of rural farmers and communities. At a macro-level, the UNCCD is particularly relevant to most of southern Africa. Large parts of the region are semi-arid (<600mm of rainfall per annum) or arid (<100mm per annum); rainfall is seasonal with long dry winters and the entire region is highly susceptible to periodic droughts, closely related to the El Nino phenomena (Gommes and Petrassi 1996).

The SAfMA notes that land degradation appears to be linked to overstocking with livestock and that there is a particularly high correspondence between degraded land and areas of communal land tenure (Biggs *et al.* 2004) – although it should be noted that in sub-Saharan Africa, the issues of semi-arid rangelands, carrying capacity and environmental degradation have been highly politicised, and there is much debate about the temporality of the apparent degradation of rangeland (see Leach *et al.* 1999). What is clear, however, is that the extensive wildlife production systems being developed by many of the CBNRM programmes are, by nature, multi-species systems occupying a range of biological niches. Theoretically these multi-species production systems reduce the pressure on rangelands compared with single species production systems (such as cattle ranching) and agro-pastoral systems (see Child 1988; Bond *et al.* 2004). The limited data available suggests that land which has reverted to wildlife production after a period of intensive single species production systems, soon shows major gains in diversity, resilience, and ecosystem function (du Toit 1999).

In terms of the UNCCD, the southern African wildlife-based CBNRM programmes aim to maintain indigenous vegetation over extensive areas[15]. If it is assumed that the conversion of arid and semi-arid land to settlement and agro-pastoral uses is a contributing factor to desertification, then it is possible to argue that the wildlife-based CBNRM programmes make a direct and positive contribution to the overall goals of the UNCCD. There are however two other benefits:

1. Areas of unsettled land or wildlife habitat can also provide communities with resource sinks that can be used in times of stress – providing that access is not restricted (see Mapedza and Bond submitted).

2. The receipt of discretionary funds at community level means that these can also be used to mitigate the effects of drought. [16]

An indirect benefit of the CBNRM programmes in terms of the 'Rio Conventions' and other multinational environmental agreements is the formation of effective community-based organisations (CBOs) (see Box 6). These CBOs become conduits through which other development and environment-based activities can be channelled.

Box 6. CBOs facilitate success in Namibia's Desertification Action Plan

Various studies of the role of community-based organisations in combating desertification in Namibia suggest that institutional development has been important for community development and governance as well as for natural resource management. An evaluation of the activities of the National Action Plan to Combat Desertification in southern Namibia found there was a higher likelihood of success in combating desertification where consistent support is focused through "a community organisational medium"

(Deutsch 2002).

6.4.2. Climate change

The total production of greenhouse gases from Africa is very small. UNEP's Global Environment Outlook 2000 cites a World Bank figure of just 7 per cent of global emissions, and under 4 per cent of carbon dioxide emissions (UNEP 2000). However, Africa (and central southern Africa in particular) is expected to suffer

---

[15] The total area of wildlife habitat being managed under CBNRM programmes in southern Africa is approximately 313,000 km2 (Cumming, 2004).

[16] Although there is little or no documented evidence of communities using wildlife money for drought relief activities, there are communities in Zimbabwe who used their wildlife revenue to buy and transport discounted maize for the poorest households (pers. experience).

some of the most severe impacts on livelihoods as a result of climate change, particularly in terms of the impacts of extreme weather conditions – droughts and floods – on agricultural production (Desanker and Magadza 2001).

The relationship between the UNFCCC and CBNRM is very similar to that of CBNRM and the UNCCD. Where CBNRM is contributing to maintenance of natural habitat, and in particular forest cover, it is effectively contributing to a reduction in greenhouse gases emission from land-use change. More importantly though, the maintenance of extensive areas of wildlife habitat, the livelihood diversification associated with involvement in wildlife conservation, and effective local institutions are critical components that will contribute to the process of adaptation to climate change (see Reid 2004).

Within the region there are community-led schemes that directly contribute to UNFCCC objectives. The Plan Vivo system, for example, aims to allow rural communities to participate in the voluntary carbon market (Orrego 2005). Plan Vivo is a set of procedures and administrative systems for managing carbon assets for small-scale farmers and community groups. A project support team maintains a database, manages a carbon trust fund, administers carbon sale agreements to farmers, and provides technical support on land-use planning, agroforestry, data collection and training. The farmers are responsible for producing and delivering the carbon services and they enter into contractual agreements with the projects for carbon service delivery. (In the Caprivi region of Namibia, conservation farming promoted in conservancies by the Living in a Finite Environment (LIFE) project is expected to have similar results in terms of reducing slash and burn agricultural practices.)

Currently, Plan Vivo has pilot sites in Uganda and Mozambique. The sites are operating at a relatively small scale, are based on voluntary carbon offsets, and are supported by donor grants. The conditions of the Kyoto Protocol – which can be technically complex and costly – do, however, constrain widespread expansion of these community schemes (Orrego 2005). Discussions are underway, however, to include "avoided deforestation" within the Clean Development Mechanism (currently only reforestation or afforestation schemes qualify for carbon payments). This would provide a major incentive for forest conservation – including for community initiatives.

7. Lessons from other regions

7.1 Community conservation in India, Central America and South East Asia

Community conservation in southern Africa is characterised by a focus on a limited range of high value (predominantly mammal) wildlife species. In other parts of the world, community conservation efforts are directed more broadly at a wide range of natural resources, at large-scale habitats, and at ecosystem services. In India, for example, there are thousands of community-conserved areas (CCAs) – natural and modified ecosystems containing significant biodiversity values, ecological services, and cultural values. These include ecosystems with minimum, as well as substantial, human influence. They are voluntarily conserved by concerned indigenous mobile and local communities through customary laws or other effective means (Pathak *et al.* 2005).

There has been an attempt in the recent past to document these community conservation initiatives but it is thought that there remain many that are still undiscovered. These initiatives range from efforts to continue traditional protection of sacred sites and revived interest and engagement of communities in protecting their natural resource catchments, to communities saving natural habitats from destructive commercial and industrial forces (see Box 7). Communities themselves have initiated many of these, while others have been supported or facilitated by external agencies. Despite the fact that the history of conservation and sustainable use in many of these areas is much older than government-managed protected areas, these areas have often been neglected or not recognised in official conservation systems and many of them face enormous threats to their existence.

At the government level, the Forest Department (which manages the majority of India's forest land) follows a system that traditionally allowed for very little community participation. In the last two decades or so however, there have been some significant moves to include and/or recognise the significance of community conservation. In contrast to the mandates of earlier forest-related policies, whose focus was maximising revenues and promoting forest-based industry, the Forest Policy of 1988 enabled the creation of space for the participation of forest-dependent people in the management of state-owned forests. The Joint Forest Management (JFM) Programme translates the participatory objectives of the 1988 Forest Policy into practice. JFM orders differ from state to state, but almost all provide for community use of resources such as NTFPs, fuelwood, and small timber from protected forest areas. The revised guidelines of February 2000 have opened up the potential for sustainable participatory management of all forests other than protected forest areas (TPCG Kalpavriksh 2005). At present, 27 out of a total of 33 states have started JFM and around 63,000 community forest

Box 7. Examples of community-conserved areas in India

- Protection of 1,800 hectares of forest by Mendha-Lekha village in Maharashtra, by Gond tribal community. Village has also achieved self-governance and assured income for all members through the year.

- Regeneration and protection of 600-700 hectares of forest by Jardhargaon village in Uttaranchal. Villagers have also re-discovered hundreds of varieties of indigenous crops and are successfully growing them organically, practising a traditional system of grassland and water management. In recent years they have also struggled to save not only the forests in their own village but in the surrounding areas, which are being destroyed by mining or hydro-electric projects.

- Protection of sea turtle eggs, hatchlings, and nesting sites by a fishing community in Kolavipaalam. Community members continue their struggle against the threats posed by sand miners whose activities are threatening the nesting sites.

- Traditional conservation of Painted Stork and globally-threatened Spot-billed Pelican nesting sites by villagers in Kokkare Bellur village, Karnataka, Veerapattu and Nellapatu in Andhra Pradesh and tens of other villages in India.

- Religious protection of the endangered Blacknecked Crane in Sangti Valley, Arunachal Pradesh by Buddhist communities.

- Community-based monitoring and enterprise by the Soliga tribals at the Biligiri Rangaswamy Temple Sanctuary, Karnataka. Vivekananda Girijan Kalyan Kendra, an NGO has helped establish an NTFP enterprise and ATREE, a scientific institute, has helped villagers carry out scientific monitoring of extracted resources.

- Community forestry being practised in several thousand villages of Orissa, without any input from the forest department. The oldest example is believed to have started in 1936. Most of these villages were faced with serious resource depletion and decided to regenerate their degrading forests.

- 600 ha of village forest in the catchment of Loktak Lake in Manipur have been regenerated by the youth of the Ronmei tribe from Tokpa Kabui village, Chandrapur district, Manipur. This community, traditionally known for its hunting skills, has also completely banned hunting of locally threatened antelope species.

Source: Pathak et al. 2004.

37

protection committees are managing over 14 million hectares of forestland. The land area under JFM is now comparable to that of India's protected area network.

Amendments to the Wildlife (Protection) Act (1972) in 2002 provided for the formation of two new categories of protected areas: conservation reserves – which the state government may declare after consultations with relevant local communities; and community reserves – areas which the local community has volunteered to conserve on private or community land. Moreover, recent decentralisation policies also have significant potential for enhancing community conservation (TPCG Kalpavriksh 2005).

In Central America, the legal and policy framework for land and natural resources is an obstacle to community conservation. Protected areas account for almost 25 per cent of the total land area of the region, and the financial hardship of most of these has resulted in limited opportunities for revenue-sharing or co-management schemes – although experience is beginning to emerge, particularly in Honduras and Belize (SICAP 2003). There are no regional or national policies that officially recognise community-conserved areas or co-management although there are some examples of these governance types, for example co-management of the Cahuita National Park in Costa Rica, and community forest concessions in the Mayan Reserve, Guatemala. There are also some well-known examples of successful community conservation for example the Community Baboon Sanctuary on community owned land or the Cockscomb Wildlife Basin Sanctuary and Jaguar Preserve in Belize, and the turtle egg hatchery in Ostional, Costa Rica and so on.

Government policies towards state-managed lands are also changing. The Managua Declaration, signed by the Central American Commission for Environment and Development (CCAD) in 2003 highlighted the need to develop protected area plans in a participatory manner – although there has been limited evidence of this policy being implemented in practice to date. A brief review of CBD country reports from Costa Rica, El Salvador and Guatemala does, however, show increasing efforts by these three governments to involve communities in the management of protected areas and buffer zones. Furthermore, the majority of protected areas fall into the IUCN management categories IV, V and VI, affording far greater potential for community involvement than the strict protection categories I and II do.

Costa Rica, for example, established a National System of Conservation Areas (SINAC) in 1995 which links private and state-owned conservation areas in order to facilitate ecosystem management that is not constrained by physical or political boundaries (Key to Costa Rica 2003). Costa Rica's 1997 biodiversity law also provides for a tax on fuel in order to compensate the owners of forested land for the environmental services they provide including:

- Reduction of greenhouse gases;
- Protection of drinking water;
- Protection of rivers that can be harnessed for hydroelectric power;
- Protection of biodiversity and its sustainable use for pharmaceuticals and science;
- Protection of ecosystems, life forms and scenic beauty.

Box 8. The Mesoamerican Biological Corridor

The end of the civil wars that plagued most of the countries of Central America in the 1970s and 80s provided the opportunity for an organised effort to set aside land for the conservation of native species of flora and fauna. In 1989, the countries of Central America formed a commission to promote and coordinate sound environmental policy throughout the isthmus.

In the early 1990s, governments entertained the idea of the 'Paseo Pantera' (Panther's Path): an unbroken strand of protected forest lands stretching along the Caribbean coast of Central America, which would guarantee the range that wild animals need in order to survive. Although this project was funded by a consortium of conservation organisations, it foundered in the face of opposition from indigenous and campesino groups. Indigenous lands often have extensive forests, and governments have rarely been concerned with giving native people legal title to them. Poor farmers often lack title as well. Both groups were aware of Central American history, throughout which elites have taken the most desirable lands and pushed native people out. They feared a land grab that would banish them, once again, from their homes.

With time, even strict conservationists came to see that it was unnecessary to prohibit all human activity in order to preserve nature. They also began to understand that large tracts of land could never be assembled if the needs of local residents were not met. In 1998, a regional group of indigenous people and farmers asserted their role in the planning of a large, unbroken habitat for native animals and plants. By this time, southern Mexico, wanting to preserve the biological riches of the Yucatan peninsula, had joined the conservation activities of Central America. Through this coalition of governments, NGOs and peoples, the 'Paseo Pantera' expanded to become the Mesoamerican Biological Corridor.

Today, the aims of the Mesoamerican Biological Corridor are:

a. To protect key biodiversity sites;

b. To connect these sites with corridors managed in such a way as to enable the movement and dispersal of animals and plants;

c. To promote forms of social and economic development in and around these areas that conserve biodiversity while being socially equitable and culturally sensitive.

Source: Key to Costa Rica 2003.

Indigenous groups are major actors in this region (see Box 8). The Association of Forest Communities of the Petén (ACOFOP) in Guatemala, for example, represents 23 organisations (cooperatives, civil society organisations and associations) involved in sustainable forest management in the Maya Biosphere Reserve in the north of the country. Here, its members manage almost a half million hectares of forest, half of which is certified by the Forest Stewardship Council (Cronkleton 2005). Along with other indigenous groups, ACOFOP has successfully tackled some of the major threats to biodiversity in the region including: the uncontrolled expansion of extensive cattle ranching, the widespread practice of shifting agriculture (slash and burn), the advance of the agricultural frontier, and forest fires.

7.2 Poverty impacts

Community-conserved areas have significant potential to contribute to poverty reduction and the objectives of the MDGs. A recent analysis (Pathak *et al.* 2005) draws on examples from across the world to illustrate that CCAs may contribute to the achievement of the MDGs in many different ways.

Many CCAs are based on the sustainable use of resources. Community efforts are not only about conservation but also concern regulated access to the conserved resources. By taking de facto control over resources where such control is not legally allowed, and demonstrating effective management, community conservation efforts meet the survival needs of some of the poorest people. In the Coron Islands of the Philippines for example, villagers claiming their customary rights have been able to prevent unregulated fishing and encroachment by outsiders. The subsequent regeneration of previously depleted resources has also provided economic benefits for the local people (Ferrari and de Vera 2003).

Conservation efforts are also providing ecologically sound economic options to local communities. Enterprises based on forest or aquatic produce, community-based ecotourism, employment in conservation and land/resource management, and so on, are examples of such initiatives. In Mendha-Lekha village in India, for example, villagers have managed to create employment opportunities throughout the year in an area where such opportunities are generally very limited. In Peru, communities are establishing biocultural heritage sites such as the Potato Park. Here, indigenous populations are reviving the traditional diversity of the potato in its place of origin, and combining this with landscape conservation, enhanced livelihoods, and protection of traditional knowledge (Pathak *et al.* 2004).

Perhaps even more importantly, CCAs can often provide an opportunity for empowering hitherto marginalised sections of society. They encourage communities and individuals to participate more confidently in social and political processes, and to confront or resist sources of exploitation more strongly. At the

Arvari River initiative in western India, for example, the river basin villages have formed an Arvari Sansad (parliament), which meets regularly to take decisions on natural resource management, sharing of benefits, inter-village disputes, and agricultural strategies – decisions which were previously made at government level (Kulhari *et al.* 2003). At Saigata village in central India, a forest conservation initiative has been led by a member of the Dalit caste, the most oppressed section of caste-based society in India. This leadership has brought the Dalit caste much greater respect within the community than any government-driven empowerment scheme. In Brazil, indigenous Kayapo communities gained political power by confronting the government over the importance of protecting the boundaries of Xingu National Park (Brockington and Igoe in press). As is the case in southern Africa, such political empowerment is often seen by communities as being, in itself, a strong motivation for community conservation (Kothari *et al.* 2000).

Box 9. Dwardi Village, India – more water, more wealth

The Dwardi Village is a good example of how a three-year village-based watershed restoration project can be an effective route to restoring vital watershed functions and increasing the productivity of local ecosystems, increasing farm income, and making available more forest products that directly benefit village livelihoods and build their local economies. Today in Dwardi, farm-based employment is available for 9-10 months of the year (compared with 3-4 months previously), and agricultural wages have doubled. More crop varieties are now grown due to extensive new irrigation, and the value of cultivated land has quadrupled. This example of village-led watershed restoration linked to sustainable rural livelihoods has been replicated in 145 villages in 24 districts of Maharashtra, India.

Source: WRI 2005.

Community conservation efforts have also helped improve the status of women. In many instances women, out of sheer desperation at the degradation of survival resources, have been forced to take natural resource management into their own hands – often with the side effect of greater respect in society in general. The Chipko movement in the Indian Himalaya is an example of how the need to protect forests from outside contractors – as well as from their own men folk – contributed significantly to a greater say for women in other village matters.

Many participating communities in the Indian JFM Programme have benefited from an increase in income through employment, sales of non timber products, and shares in the final harvests (RUPFOR 2002: 37):

- 21.58 million person days of employment were generated in just six states in 2000-01; 40 million person days of employment were created through JFM under the Andhra Pradesh Forestry Project (1994-2000).

- Rs 1 million (US $21,000) was spent on each micro-plan under the Maharashtra Forestry Project.

- In four states, forest protection committees (FPCs) received around Rs 62.59 million (US $13 million) through benefit-sharing mechanisms during 2000-01. In the state of West Bengal, it is estimated that on average each FPC has received about Rs 70,000 (US$ 1,500) as share in timber revenue.

- At the end of 2000-01, total community funds under JFM were Rs 557.09 million (US$ 11.6 million) in seven states.

Box 10. PES in Costa Rica

In Costa Rica, the government has paid landowners for forest conservation services since 1996. The Fondo Nacional de Financiamiento Forestal (FONAFIFO) pays forest owners for reforestation and forest conservation on long-term (10-15 year) contracts, using funds from a national fuel tax and contributions from private companies. By the end of 2001 nearly 4,500 contracts had been agreed, covering 250,000 hectares and worth US$50 million. Applications were underway for a further 800,000 hectares. In the Huetar Norte region, participants in a carbon sequestration scheme believe that, in addition to the cash income, the payment scheme has helped strengthen community associations – including a small producers' agricultural association and a wood development association. It is also thought that tourism has taken off in the area as a result of the improved forest landscape. Producers in the scheme are, however, expected to have officially-recognised land title documents – a barrier to many poor people. Efforts are made to target smallholders, with plots as small as 1 ha being eligible for the scheme, but evidence shows that the majority of the benefits flow to large landowners with more than 70 ha. Furthermore, a requirement that land should remain idle while an application is being processed – which may take up to 12 months – serves as a large disincentive for the poorest landowners.

Source: Grieg-Gran and Bishop 2004.

Despite these apparent successes, one of the main criticisms of JFM has been that it might actually be detrimental to existing community systems by attempting to impose homogeneity onto some very complex heterogeneous systems. The revised JFM guidelines do not mention decentralisation of governance and the role of "Panchayati Raj" (local self-governance) Institutions (PRIs). In addition, some commentators argue that JFM has not given enough attention to the protection of indigenous knowledge and the equitable sharing of benefits from its wider use (TPCG Kalpavriksh 2005).

In Central America, despite the challenges, community conservation projects and programmes across the region are generating both direct and indirect financial benefits for rural people. In most cases this income is purely supplementary to other forms of household income such as agricultural or wage labour (Gutierrez *et al.* 2000). From other projects there are specific cases of the commoditisation of wildlife and other natural resources (eggs, meat, skins etc.).

Central America has, however, provided a model for many of the 'payments for environmental services' (PES) schemes that are emerging as a key mechanism for enhancing the local capture of biodiversity benefits. The MA highlights PES as a promising incentive mechanism, and experience from Costa Rica in particular is promising (Box 10). The basic concept is to create positive economic incentives for landowners to optimise environmental services including carbon sequestration, wildlife habitat, watershed protection and so on. There are, however, some concerns regarding the equity impacts of such schemes – the danger is that the more powerful members of a community are likely to be in the best position to benefit from them, while the poorest and more marginalised members may not be able to participate because they lack clear land title and may even suffer detrimental impacts due to restricted access to previously open access resources.

7.3 Contributions to biodiversity conservation

In India (signatory to the CBD since 1993) the majority of work in meeting the goals of the CBD has been directed towards *in situ* conservation of biodiversity. Community conservation contributes to this. The implementation of JFM, for example has increased the overall forest cover by 3,896 km² and dense forest cover by 10,098 km² (RUPFOR 2002).

CCAs often provide corridors and linkages for animal and gene movement, sometimes between two or more officially protected areas. In the Himalayan state of Uttaranchal in India, for example, two critical protected areas (the Nanda Devi National Park and Biosphere Reserve, and the Askot Sanctuary) are linked by hundreds of square kilometres of community forest land managed under the traditional "van panchayat" (village council) system (Foundation for Ecological Security 2003). Together they form a contiguous forest swathe of almost 300,000 ha (3,000 km²), which would make it one of India's biggest protected areas if the village forests were recognised as equivalent to formal protected areas (Pathak *et al.* 2005).

Significant among community conservation efforts are sacred spaces that have historically been conserved by communities for spiritual/cultural reasons and have today become important reservoirs of biodiversity. Most common among them are sacred groves, which are patches of forest where harvesting or any other kind of human intervention is prohibited. These are found in all parts of the country and are known by a variety of different names. Malhotra *et al.* (2000) estimate that although there are 13,720 reported sacred groves, the total number could be anywhere between 100,000 and 150,000. Most sacred groves contain rich floral and faunal biodiversity. A sacred grove in the state of Kerala with an area of only

Table 4. Ecological impacts of CCAs in South Asia

Type of initiative	Ecological impact	Examples[17]
Traditional protection of sacred sites	Protection (often total) of forests, grasslands, tanks	Several thousand in India and Bangladesh, usually small in extent
Traditional protection of sacred species	Protection of key species	Bluebull (nilgai), rhesus macaque, and *Ficus* spp., all over India; blackbuck and other species in Bishnoi community area, Rajasthan, India; *Ficus* spp., *Madhuca indica*, *Prosopis cineraria*, other trees in many countries
Traditional sustainable-use practices for habitats	Conservation of habitats such as village tanks, pastures and forests, and wildlife species resident in them	Kokkare Bellur, India; 'bugiyals' (pastures) in Indian Himalaya; several marine sites with traditionally regulated fisheries, in India and elsewhere
Traditional sustainable-use practices for species	Conservation of wildlife species along with, or independent, of their habitats	Trees like *Madhuca indica*, harvested with great restraint in many parts of tribal India; hunting restraints for several species
Recent initiatives to revive degraded habitats and sustainably use them	Regeneration of forests, grasslands and ther ecosystems, and of species dependent on them	Several million hectares of forest lands in India (Joint Forest Management or community-initiated) and several hundred thousand hectares in Nepal and Bhutan community forests
Recent initiatives to conserve and/ or sustainably use relatively intact ecosystems	Conservation of important ecosystems and their resident species, reduction in threats to them	Mendha-Lekha, India; Annapurna Conservation Area, Nepal; Muthurajawela Marsh and Lagoon, Sri Lanka; Eco-development at Periyar Tiger Reserve, India; community wildlife and forest reserves in Nagaland, India
Recent initiatives at sustainable (consumptive and non-consumptive) use of species	Revival of threatened populations of wildlife, e.g. ibex; and reduction in over-exploitation, e.g. of plant and aquatic species	Hushey, Pakistan; Rekawa, Sri Lanka; at Biligiri Rangaswamy Temple Sanctuary, India
Resistance to marine destructive commercial forces	Reduction or elimination of factors threatening ecosystems and species	Protection of Indian coastline and areas by traditional fisherfolk, from destructive fishing and aquaculture; several movements against big 'development' projects in several countries; movement against mining in Sariska Tiger Reserve, India

Source: Adapted from Kothari *et al.* 2000

1.4 km^2 harbours 722 angiosperm species as compared to a protected forest area in the same state which had 960 angiosperm species in 90 km^2.

Sacred landscapes are an expanded form of the sacred grove concept and have within them several ecosystems, both human-made and natural. In the state of Sikkim, the residents consider the valley of Rathong Chu below Mount Khangchendzonga as sacred, and a hydroelectric project was stopped on the basis of this belief. There are also many wetland habitats which are conserved for their sacred value, but which in the process conserve many aquatic species of fauna and flora (TPCG Kalpavriksh 2005).

Watershed protection is one of the most common motivations for CCAs. Several dozen villages in the arid state of Rajasthan, in western India, have regenerated and conserved forests in catchment areas and established small-scale water harvesting structures, aware that such measures will provide greater water security than any massive engineering interventions. As a result, a previously dried up river, the Arvari, has come back to life. Hundreds of initiatives across India are based on similar motivations, from the traditional 'Safety Forests' of Mizoram to the new 'Village Forest Reserves' in Nagaland. Secure or enhanced availability of ecological services also provide a tangible opportunity to enhance economic benefits. In the Arvari River example mentioned above, the increased reliability and amount of water has resulted in a significant increase in agricultural production (Pathak *et al.* 2005). Table 4 summarises the wide range of ecological impacts of CCAs in India and across South Asia.

Unlike the situation in southern Africa, community conservation in India has also focused on domesticated biodiversity. 'Beej Bachao Andolan' (the Save the Seeds Movement) is one of the many networks and organisations (which include tens of thousands of farmers) that are trying to save agricultural biodiversity (TPCG, Kalpavriksh 2005). In this case, a collective of farmers from the Himalayan state of Uttaranchal collected a large diversity of seeds in an attempt to save indigenous plants from the onslaught of new hybrid varieties. The movement has been successful in conserving *(in situ)* several hundred traditional varieties including wheat, oats, amranthus, buckwheat, and corn etc.).

Efforts to link biodiversity conservation to agricultural livelihoods have also met with some success in Central America. Conservation International, for example, promotes the concept of 'conservation coffee' and works directly with farmers to promote environmentally responsible growing practices such as water and soil conservation, crop diversification, and chemical fertilizer and pesticide reduction that help protect the surrounding forest, streams and wildlife. [18]

---

[17] This is not an exhaustive list of examples, but only some selected at random
[18] http://www.scienceblog.com/community/older/2004/2/20041736.shtml

Box 11. Community fisheries and equity in India

Communities living along the coasts and who are dependent on aquatic resources have developed traditional systems to ensure equitable access to resources. In the Allepey and Ernakulam districts of the state of Kerala, there is a system for distributing income amongst fisherfolk who practise canoe and encircling net fishery. This half a century-old system ensures income to permanent, semi-permanent, and also temporary crew on a boat, even if they have not done productive work on a particular trip. In another system on the coast of Tamil Nadu, traditional fishing councils regulate fishing efforts in inshore waters. At the Pulicat Lake in Andhra Pradesh, entitlements are granted to eligible members of a particular community for fishing in certain designated fishing grounds. This system ensures compatible fishing rights and avoids conflict.

Source: TPCG, Kalpavriksh 2005.

One of the root causes of biodiversity loss and the decline of biodiversity-dependent livelihoods in India has been the inequities in access to resources, use of these resources, and the sharing of benefits derived from them. In terms of agro-biodiversity, measures to protect traditional knowledge have yet to be put in place and there has been little recognition of the role of marginalised groups – particularly women and pastoralists. Other than JFM (to some extent), there is no attempt to establish a clear legal or institutional mechanism to secure improved common property resource access for biodiversity-dependent people, and no active mechanism has been put in place to resolve issues related to land rights of forest dwellers. The recent Scheduled Tribes (Recognition of Forest Rights) Bill (2005) may help in changing the situation, but it is difficult to evaluate this until it becomes an Act and is implemented. Decentralisation of power, scheduled to take place in all states through the empowerment of the Gram Sabha,[19] is happening very slowly. Furthermore, the state government has divested the 'panchayats'[20] of their control over grazing lands for distribution among the landless. This may be beneficial from an equity point of view, but could adversely impact biodiversity and local livelihoods depending on who gains control and how the land is managed.

---

[19] All men and women in the village who are above 18 years of age form the Gram Sabha. The Gram Sabha meets twice a year. Meetings of the Gram Sabha are convened to ensure the development of the people through their participation and mutual co-operation.
[20] Gram Panchayats are local government bodies at the village level in India.

7.4 Community conservation, desertification and climate change – experience from India and South East Asia

It is clear from the objectives of the UNCCD that communities are recognised to play a crucial role in addressing the issues of degradation and desertification. They have been identified as primary beneficiaries as well as key players. However, traditional methods of combating degradation and desertification are rapidly eroding without adequate official recognition and legal backing; nevertheless, in some cases they still prevail, or have been incorporated into government schemes.

Box 12. Traditional water management in India

In many parts of the Tehri region in the western Himalaya, 'pani panchayat' (village water councils) are responsible for a traditional system of irrigation that regulates water during periods of need and ensures equitable distribution amongst local farmers. In parts of Rajasthan, there are also several villages that have regenerated and conserved forests in catchments and established water-harvesting structures for greater water security. A previously dried-up river, the Arvari, has actually been resurrected as a result of this, leading to a significant increase in agriculture production in the area.

Source: Pathak et al. 2004.

47

India has good reasons to be concerned about the impacts of climate change, primarily because it has a large population that is heavily dependent on climate-sensitive sectors (like agriculture and forestry) to meet their livelihood requirements. Changes in water availability as a result of glacial recession will have an impact on food security – both as a result of decreased agricultural productivity and degradation of natural ecosystems. The livelihoods of coastal communities will be impacted by sea level rises and the increased frequency of natural disasters. It is perhaps for this reason that community conservation has made, and can make, the greatest contribution to the UNFCCC with regard to vulnerability, assessment and adaptation.

The use of community conservation as a carbon sequestration mechanism is becoming increasingly common in many other regions of the world. In South East Asia, for example, the Canadian Climate Change Development Fund is supporting a number of initiatives (CIDA Forestry Advisors Network 2004):

• In Indonesia, the Forest Resources Management for Carbon Sequestration (FORMACS) Project works with 38 forest-dwelling communities in the Nunukan District of East Kalimantan Province. It promotes sustainable livelihoods through sustainable agriculture, agro-forestry, and sustainable forest management practices for the maintenance of existing carbon stocks and for the sequestration of atmospheric carbon.

- In East Timor (Timor Leste) a similar project promotes CBNRM in the Manatuto and Aileu districts to maintain the carbon stocks stored in the forest vegetation and to increase the sequestration of atmospheric carbon. It simultaneously supports local farmers in adopting land-use practices to improve livelihood security.

- In Indonesia, projects in Central Kalimantan and Sumatra are intended to promote community-based approaches for managing peatlands and incorporation of these approaches into the national climate change policy and implementation framework. Peatlands are a particularly significant ecosystem for climate change – if maintained in their natural state they sequester and store atmospheric carbon, thus mitigating greenhouse gas emissions. However, if they are disturbed by drainage and burning, the stored carbon is released into the atmosphere contributing to the greenhouse effect. The peat swamp forests are also rich storehouses of plant and animal biodiversity. Sustainable forest management will not only have a positive impact on carbon sequestration and storage and community livelihoods, it will also have a positive impact on conserving the forest biodiversity.

Box 13. Water storage in Ladakh

In the high altitude cold desert of Ladakh, the approximate rainfall between May and July is 50 mm. Water from melted snow provides sustenance for the inhabitants; the agricultural season commences with the melting of snows. However, if melting is delayed there is no water for the agricultural season and sowing is delayed. The community here has developed a traditional water storage system. Farmers from time immemorial have attempted to create 'artificial glaciers' (or ice blocks) by diverting water from streams located at the base of mountains. By doing this they ensure that these blocks melt earlier than the water from the glaciers, thus providing water for irrigation at the right time. The Department of Rural Development in Ladakh has adapted this idea and used appropriate technology to create 'artificial glaciers' which have proved to be successful and cost-effective.

Source: Norphel 2001 and Athavale 2003.

Elsewhere, CARE is promoting community forestry and agroforestry over 80,000 ha – an initiative that is expected to sequester over 11 million tonnes of carbon, and the Biodiversifix Project in Costa Rica is regenerating 135,000 ha of rainforest and is expecting to sequester over 15 million tonnes (WRI 2006).

Overall, these schemes show exceptional promise with huge potential for expansion and replication. Community Forestry International (CFI undated) notes that "The carbon sequestration value of community-based forest protection is substantial. One study reported that carbon levels of 3 to 5 metric tons per hectare in scrubland can rise to 60 to 90 metric tons per hectare in regenerating forests after 25 years of protection". As discussed above, if the current moves to include avoided deforestation in the Kyoto Protocol, (as suggested to the latest Conference of Parties of the UNFCC by Papua New Guinea and Costa Rica on behalf of the Coalition for Rainforest Nations[21]), are accepted, then the potential is even greater.

[49]

---

[21] A group of 10 developing countries with significant rainforest resources.

8

Part Three:

Conclusions and recommendations
8. The role of community conservation – conceptual and empirical limitations

The Millennium Ecosystem Assessment emphasises the inter-relationship between ecosystem health and human well-being. According to the MA conceptual framework, it is the various services that ecosystems provide that contribute to human well-being (security, health, basic materials for a good life, good social relations and freedom of choice and action). Biodiversity underpins the delivery of these ecosystem services and hence biodiversity conservation is essential for securing human well-being.

Evidence from this review shows that community conservation can contribute to human well-being both directly – for example, through income-earning opportunities, local empowerment, or increased security of resource access – and indirectly, though biodiversity conservation. The extent to which the impact on biodiversity from community conservation contributes to the maintenance or improvement of ecosystem services is, however, difficult to assess. In southern Africa, community conservation has become closely associated with high profile donor-funded initiatives such as CAMPFIRE in Zimbabwe, the conservancy programme in Namibia, and ADMADE and LIRDP in Zambia – all of which focus predominantly on species (particularly large mammal) conservation. Species conservation is only one of eleven responses to biodiversity loss that the MA identifies. It is an essential activity – but is insufficient unless linked to broader habitat-based initiatives. Habitat and ecosystem restoration activities – another key response – do happen in southern Africa but tend to be a secondary focus, lacking the support that species-based initiatives receive. This report highlights the significant donor funding that is channelled towards community conservation in the region, but with very little recognition of the lower profile, often 'home-grown' initiatives that focus on fisheries, eco-agriculture, watershed conservation and so on. In other regions such as in Central America, South East Asia and India, community conservation initiatives are more broadly associated with the management of forests and other ecosystems – rather than large mammals – and therefore inevitably address conservation at a much wider scale.

In many cases, community conservation has demonstrated considerable success in restoring previously degraded habitat, reintroducing locally extinct species, supporting state-run protected areas, and capturing benefits for local communities. In the majority of cases, however, community conservation initiatives remain small-scale, isolated, and not mainstreamed within the 'formal' conservation sector. Not only is community participation limited within the conservation sector, but conservation is rarely integrated with other natural resource sectors – including agriculture, fisheries and forestry – although promising signs are shown in the increasing number of 'co-management' arrangements that are beginning to emerge [22].

Most of the information and analyses of the impacts of community conservation are limited by being either site-specific case studies or based on limited time-series analyses. Impacts measured through site-specific case studies cannot be extrapolated to either the project or the programme level, let alone the regional or global level (Magome and Fabricius 2004). Similarly, limited time-series analyses do not allow significant causal relationships to be developed between indicators and changes in management practices. The influence and the role of donor funding often complicates an already difficult set of cause-effect relationships (Frost and Bond submitted).

In terms of the impact of community conservation on poverty, it is useful to distinguish between poverty mitigation and poverty reduction or elimination. The evidence reviewed in this report suggests that to date, community conservation is primarily to be understood as a poverty mitigation strategy. It is however important to emphasise that site-specific impacts range from the very marginal to the quite substantial. WRI (2005) argues, however, that ecosystems can and should be managed to fight poverty, and recommends four steps to realise the wealth of the poor:

1. More income through better ecosystem management.
2. Getting the governance right: empowering the poor to profit from nature.
3. Commercialising ecosystem goods and services.
4. Augmenting nature's income stream by developing systems for payments for environmental services.

In many cases, the achievements of community conservation may fall well short of the expectations of both communities and advocates. The latter group have often been guilty of extrapolating from individual case studies and of poly-valency (Jones and Murphree 2004). In many cases this can be attributed to their desire to both challenge conventional conservation approaches and to attract donor funds necessary to support pilot community conservation activities. At the same time, however, community conservation cannot be expected to be a panacea. At the local level, community conservation can help address the direct drivers of biodiversity loss – habitat change, invasive species, over-exploitation, pollution and even, as this review illustrates, climate change. At the national and global level however, the main drivers of biodiversity loss and ecosystem change are way beyond the reach of community action – these include demographic pressure (and the implication this has for urbanisation, resource consumption, and food production), globalisation processes, economic and trade policies, and so on. Without adequate attention to

[22] See Borrini-Feyarabend *et al*. 'Sharing Power' for a detailed review of co-management.

these issues, of course, community conservation will only ever be a marginal activity.

Associated with the unrealistically high expectations for community conservation is the notion that sustainable development ('win-win') opportunities always exist. In reality, opportunities in which it is possible to fulfil both conservation and development objectives may be limited. As we highlighted in Section 3, the MA is clear that 'win-wins' are highly elusive. A more realistic scenario is where trade-offs between the two sets of objectives are needed. These trade-offs need to be negotiated between stakeholders with an understanding of their short-, medium- and long-term implications.

Too often (and for the purposes of analysis) community conservation and conventional conservation approaches are considered as discrete alternatives. The reality of conservation and development activities is that they are taking place in complex and often rapidly changing political, social, economic, and even biological landscapes. Within this complexity there are justifications not only for conventional conservation approaches (i.e. protection of areas with high biodiversity) but also for sustainable use and the suite of options that constitute community conservation. We would argue however that there are some systems, for example the communal lands of southern Africa, where there is no alternative to community conservation approaches. The residents of these largely semi-arid areas, which are only marginally suitable for agriculture, depend on natural resources for their livelihoods. In these areas conservation or sustainable use of natural resources is a priority which precludes any return to the coercive policies that characterised colonial periods and which are often associated with conventional conservation measures.

Community conservation cannot solve the huge and interlinked challenges the global community faces in terms of poverty reduction and biodiversity loss. Without local action, however, the international targets set within the CBD and the MDGs are likely to be at best irrelevant, and most likely unattainable. A number of recent studies and analyses have now identified the links between poverty reduction and biodiversity loss and highlighted the role of governance in addressing both. Community conservation provides crucial lessons in participatory governance of natural resources – lessons that are already being used in many countries to resolve previously intractable conflicts between official conservation agencies and local rights-holders and stakeholders. Given appropriate support, community conservation could undoubtedly achieve more than it does currently. Unleashing this potential, moving beyond the small, the isolated, and the site-specific will, however, require considerable reorientation of both donor and government policy. One thing that is clear is that there is no 'one size fits all' solution. Site-specific situations and circumstances need site-specific rules, regulations and institutions. This points towards a system of conservation where decisions about who manages the resources, how and why, depend on the local situation rather than uniform national legal requirements.

9. Conclusions and recommendations: enhancing the contribution of community conservation to achieving the MDGs and MEAs

9

A. Community conservation and ecosystem services

Experience from different regions of the world shows that community conservation can, and does, make a contribution to the maintenance or restoration of critical ecosystem services that support life on Earth. However, addressing ecosystem degradation requires multiple responses and many community conservation efforts focus on only one strategy (for example species conservation) and/or are isolated from mainstream conservation efforts such as national protected area networks.

> Enhancing the contribution of community conservation requires a broadening of the current donor-driven concepts of community conservation to recognise the many traditional practices of local communities that contribute to ecosystem management, as well as better integration of community efforts within the formal conservation sector and other natural resource sectors.

53

B. Community conservation and the MDGs

Biodiversity conservation can make a significant contribution to achieving many of the MDGs (see Box 1) and community efforts to conserve biodiversity are part of this. Biodiversity is only specifically mentioned in MDG7 –'Ensure Environmental Sustainability', where protected area coverage is a key indicator. In the majority of cases, however, CCAs are ignored when protected area coverage is calculated – despite being recognised by IUCN as a legitimate governance type. One exception to this is Madagascar, which has drawn up plans to use a range of governance types, including a large number of CCAs, in its efforts to increase its protected area coverage, and to 'democratise' the governance of PAs in general. [23]

> National governments may soon be expected to produce country-level MDG strategies. Recognising the role of biodiversity conservation in the achievement of the MDGs is a challenge in itself, but a significant step forward is to start with MDG7. CCAs – including indigenous territories, communal lands and sacred groves – should be given the necessary recognition and support to complement more 'traditional' protected areas. Central to this is the need to identify, and increase support for, effective local organisations in order that they can fulfil their potential of balancing conservation and development priorities.

[23] Guy Suzon Ramagason, personal communication, 2005.

C. Community conservation and the CBD

There are clear links between the principles and approaches of community conservation and the objectives and provisions of the CBD – promoting sustainable use of biodiversity, benefit-sharing, community involvement, decentralisation, and an incentive-based approach to conservation. Moreover, the ecosystem approach of the CBD emphasises decentralisation to the lowest appropriate unit of management. In reality, however, while community conservation may contribute to some of the objectives of the CBD, community involvement in the CBD – and indeed most international processes – is very limited. Indigenous knowledge, for example, is generally not well received by scientific bodies (perhaps with the exception of the Working Group on Article 8j which covers traditional knowledge). [24]

> Mechanisms need to be put in place at the national level whereby local communities can participate in decision-making processes within the CBD (and other MEAs). Community conservation is not just about the practical involvement of communities in conservation activities, but also their full and active participation in conservation planning and policy-making. Annex 2 provides an example of how this is happening in northern Canada.

54

D. Community conservation and the role of donors

There is significant donor investment in community conservation – particularly in southern Africa. Many commentators argue, however, that in many cases donor funds have overloaded what were previously sustainable, local initiatives and made them over-dependent on continued support. Largely driven by three-year project cycles, many donors pulled out of community conservation initiatives at the end of the 'project' and the initiative ground to a halt. The recent move by most official development assistance agencies towards direct budget support means that the project funding approach is now becoming less common (although the other side of the coin is that so too is funding for local groups). Nevertheless projects still exist outside of official development assistance – funded by conservation NGOs, GEF and so on. The timescales needed for the effects of community conservation efforts to become apparent are generally way beyond the project and programme timetables of most funding agencies.

---

[24] Poverty and Conservation Learning Group, Meeting Report, December 2005 (unpublished).

It is important that donors (including conservation and development organisations) recognise the importance of process – the time that it takes to make robust changes to the organisations and institutions that manage natural resources, and the way that resources are managed themselves.[25] Donors also need to think about the most appropriate role for them in community conservation. Given the changes in aid modalities, this might mean – for development agencies – exploring how community approaches can be mainstreamed into sector-wide initiatives, or what mechanisms can best facilitate investment in local environmental assets. Getting the policy and institutional framework right is critical if investing in conservation is to benefit the poor. This implies: the need for strong and secure resource and property rights to enable community institutions to function effectively; access for the poor to credit and insurance to help overcome "short-termism"; removal of perverse subsidies in rich countries; and the development of markets in environmental assets.   *(Pearce 2005).*

E. Community conservation and national policy coordination

In the different regions examined, and particularly in southern Africa, community conservation has been led by resource-specific policy reform. This has resulted in inconsistent and often completely contradictory policy environments for community-based organisations. A good example of this is from Zimbabwe, where forestry legislation remained strongly rooted in a colonial approach while wildlife policy devolved rights and responsibilities to producer communities (Nhira *et al.* 1998). This is symptomatic of the general lack of joined-up government and sectoral coordination that prevails at national and international level. Ministries governing land and resource planning are generally absent from CBD processes, (particularly in developing country delegations) and likewise environment and natural resource ministries are often absent from debates on poverty reduction.

Successful community conservation needs a coherent and holistic policy rather than piecemeal policy reform. The Millennium Ecosystem Assessment provides a framework for linking biodiversity conservation and poverty reduction efforts. Responding to this framework at the national level will necessitate inter-sectoral communication and coordination. Similarly, national MDG strategies will require consideration of the links between environmental sustainability and poverty reduction.

---

[25] The long-term investment by NORAD in the Luangwa Valley is recognition of the challenges that are associated with community conservation.

F. Community conservation and project implementation

A major constraint identified by this and other reviews of community conservation is the paucity of data on their conservation and development impacts. However, without objective, multi-site analyses of both the performance of community conservation, community resource managers and their supporters will find it increasingly difficult to maintain their arguments. The paucity of data will also mean that facilitators will lose the opportunity to adapt programmes and projects in order to maximise their success.

> Successful community conservation needs programme and project monitoring that demonstrates impact beyond site-specific case studies. Involving local communities in monitoring their achievements can also be an effective way of learning quickly from mistakes and engendering a sense of empowerment and pride.

G. Community conservation and professionalism

Community conservation is being facilitated in dynamic and complex environments. Generally, developing countries (particularly in sub-Saharan Africa) are characterised by critical shortages of skilled personnel. Those who have been trained tend to have been educated in tertiary institutes which reward specialisation in a single discipline. Similarly, their practical experience upon entering the workplace is more than likely to be in a resource-specific ministry or department.

> Mainstreaming community conservation requires that it becomes a standard part of conservation education. Training institutes need to offer multi-disciplinary courses or modules that give participants a breadth of understanding about community conservation, its potential and challenges, in order to produce skilled facilitators and administrators.

H. Community conservation and the market

The development of community conservation coincided with structural reforms that emphasised the role of the market both in development and conservation activities. While community conservation involves the commoditisation of resources and incentives for changing management practices, communities themselves seldom benefit from the full value of the resource. In southern Africa particularly, this means that attempts to manage wildlife habitat will be severely constrained by the potentially higher returns from other agro-pastoral land uses. Perverse incentives that support some forms of land use (e.g. agricultural subsidies) and discourage others (e.g. trade bans on wildlife and wildlife products) distort the market and prevent local communities from capturing the true value of biological resources. In other cases however, schemes where communities are paid for environmental services – including biodiversity conservation, carbon sequestration, or watershed protection – have generated significant benefits (e.g. in the form of cash incomes, increased security of land tenure, and strengthened community institutions) although the impacts on poorer members of the community are less clear (Grieg-Gran and Bishop 2004).

> Successful community conservation must allow natural resource managers to derive a fair market return on their investment. This requires eliminating perverse incentives, including market-distorting subsidies and other trade interventions. Payments for ecosystem services – including biodiversity, watersheds, or carbon – show significant potential in providing positive, direct incentives for conservation but require more attention (particularly to equity impacts), experimentation and support.

I. Community conservation and land reform (South Africa and Namibia only)

Within southern Africa, the only two countries that still have dual agricultural systems divided along racial lines are South Africa and Namibia. In both countries there are major programmes to address these inequalities by returning land to indigenous black farmers. Both countries are also characterised by the rapid growth of wildlife production on commercial land. In the Limpopo Province of South Africa it is estimated that more than 50 per cent of the commercial farmers are now wildlife producers. If wildlife ranching works for private landowners it can also work for communities. Land restitution and resettlement policies present major opportunities for investing in wildlife-based CBNRM.

> The resettlement programmes of South Africa and Namibia represent a major opportunity to transfer a successful land-use change from a commercial context to a community-based management system. In order to be successful, facilitators will need to draw lessons, both the positive and negative, from the wildlife-based CBNRM programmes of southern Africa.

57

Annex 1: Synopsis of the major wildlife-based CBNRM programmes in southern Africa

The CAMPFIRE programme in **Zimbabwe** used existing legislation to devolve "appropriate authority" over wildlife to rural district councils (RDCs) and developed policy guidelines that provided for further devolution to sub-district administrative units called wards. Although there have been attempts to diversify the suite of resources managed by communities under CAMPFIRE, the programme remains heavily reliant on RDCs entering into contracts with private hunting companies, and to some extent with tourism lodge operators, in order to generate income for community development. In general, RDCs have tended to hold on to large portions of the income from wildlife and tourism and have not devolved rights to the ward level. Recently there has been severe erosion of economic incentives due to hyper-inflation (Mapedza and Bond submitted). Policy planners in **Namibia** were able to learn from the CAMPFIRE approach and developed legislation that gave rights over wildlife directly to self-identifying communities called 'conservancies' (Jones and Murphree 2001). The first Namibian conservancy was registered in 1998 and there are now 44 conservancies, covering more than 10,500,000 ha.

As in Zimbabwe and Namibia, the development of CBNRM in the rest of the region has been shaped by the political, economic, historical, and social contexts of each country, resulting in a variety of policy approaches (Jones and Murphree 2001). The implementation of CBNRM in **Botswana** was driven initially by the USAID-funded Natural Resource Management Programme (NRMP), which helped develop some of the policy approaches and CBNRM guidelines, and piloted CBNRM activities with local communities (Rozemeijer 2003). The NRMP ran from 1989-1999. Implementation of CBNRM in Botswana focuses on mobilising local communities to form trusts so they can gain quotas from the wildlife department and enter into joint venture agreements for trophy hunting or photographic tourism with the private sector. By 2003, 10 years after the first trust was awarded a hunting quota, there were 46 registered trusts covering 100 villages (Rozemeijer 2003).

CBNRM in **Mozambique** is being implemented against the background of a country emerging from two decades of war, and the effects of centrally-planned economic and political strategies. According to Anstey (2001), the absence of a strong state and the presence of many donor agencies have led to a variety of implementation approaches to CBNRM in Mozambique. CBNRM is mainly based on forestry rather than wildlife resources although a pilot project called Tchuma Tchato paved the way for the establishment of other CBNRM activities related to wildlife and tourism. Legislation enabling communities to enter into contracts with the private sector for harvesting of forest products and wildlife, and securing community land rights under national legislation, has been another entry point for the implementation of CBNRM (Nhantumbo et al. in preparation).

Two main wildlife-based CBNRM programmes have emerged in **Zambia** (Jones 2004a). The ADMADE Programme was initiated in the mid 1980s as a national programme but has focused mainly on Game Management Areas in the Luangwa Valley, around Kafue National Park, and in the lower Zambezi Valley. It is based on revenue-sharing according to a formula set by government policy.

The Luangwa Integrated Rural Development Project (LIRDP) was initiated in the Lupande GMA in the Luangwa Valley in 1988. The initial design was similar to ADMADE but also aimed to link wildlife revenues with integrated rural development. The project was changed in 1996 to focus on wildlife and to introduce a greater share of income to communities and a greater degree of village-level decision-making (by the village action group). As a result 80% of wildlife based revenues earned in the Lupande GMA were devolved to VAGs (Child, 2004b). Between 1996 and 2000, the community conservation activities in Luangwa demonstrated the benefits of substantive devolution in both development and conservation achievements (opp. cit). Further evolution of the community conservation programme was initially hampered by the suspension of international trophy hunting by the Government of Zambia. This meant that meaningful revenue to village action groups (VAGs) ceased and there was little motivation to maintain the institutional and organisational framework together with the conservation and development activities that had been built up over the previous four to six years. Currently there are plans for a sixth phase of support for community conservation and development activities in Luangwa through the Norwegian Government. The next phase of this long running support to the Luangwa will see the rehabilitation of community conservation activities.

In **South Africa** wildlife-based CBNRM on communal land is rarely an option because game species have largely disappeared from community areas. As a result, the main focus of community involvement in wildlife conservation is linked to relationships with protected areas (Jones and Murphree 2004). Under land restitution laws, communities have regained land in the Kruger National Park and in the South African part of the Kgalagadi Transfrontier Park, and are gaining income through hunting and tourism. In the Richtersveld National Park, South African National Parks rents the land from the local community and manages it under a contract. In other areas the focus is on developing good park/neighbour relationships and exploring options such as allowing resource harvesting inside protected areas, and revenue sharing.

59

Annex 2: Local participation in management of Canada's wildlife resources.

Canada's Wildlife Management Advisory Council (WMAC) was established in 1988 as a result of the *Western Arctic (Inuvialuit) Settlement Act,* which arose out of the 1984 Inuvialuit Final Agreement (IFA). The Council consists of two members appointed by the Inuvialuit Game Council, one member appointed by the Minister of the Environment of Canada, one member appointed by the Yukon Territorial Government, and an independent chairperson. The Council provides advice to the appropriate minister on all matters relating to wildlife policy and the management, regulation and administration of wildlife, habitat, and harvesting for the Yukon North Slope. Since its beginnings, the Council has been an active and effective supporter of cooperative management on the Yukon's North Slope. (See www.taiga.net/wmac)

The Yukon North Slope is an area of special conservation status and has two Inuvialuit, one federal, and one territorial government. In practice, the Council's activities include: defining research and conservation needs; reviewing policy and legislation, and research and development projects in the region; advising on allocations of funding; developing park management plans for the two parks in the region; and recommending quotas for harvested species. A practical example of cooperative species management is the Porcupine Caribou Management Board – which has representatives from governments and from all the Canadian user communities (Inuvialuit, Gwich'in and Yukon First Nation) for this herd, which is the main traditional food for several communities in the Yukon and Northwest Territories, and of huge cultural importance. (See http://www.taiga.net/pcmb/updates_12.html)

References

Adams, W.M. and Hulme, D. (2001). 'Conservation and Communities: Changing Narratives, Policies and Practices in African Conservation', pp. 9-23 in Hulme, D. and Murphree, M. (eds.) *African Wildlife and Livelihoods: the promise and performance of community conservation.* James Currey. Oxford.

Adams, J.S. and McShane, T.O. (1992). *The Myth of Wild Africa: Conservation Without Illusion.* W. W. Norton and Co. New York - London.

Anderson, J., Bryceson, D., Campbell, B., Chitundu, D., Clarke, J., Drinkwater, M., Fakir, S., Frost, P.G.H., Gambiza, J., Grundy, I., Hagmann, J., Jones, B., Jones, G. W., Kowero, G., Luckert, M., Mortimore, M., Phiri, A. D. K., Potgieter, P., Shackleton, S., and Williams, T. (2004). *Chance, Change and Choice in Africa's Drylands: A new perspective on policy priorities.* CIFOR. Bogor, Indonesia.

Angelsen, A. and Wunder, S. (2003). *Exploring the Forest-Poverty Link: Key concepts, issues and research implications.* (CIFOR Occasional Paper No. 40). CIFOR. Bogor, Indonesia.

Anstey, S. (2001). 'Necessarily Vague: The political economy of community conservation in Mozambique' in Hulme, D. and Murphree, M. (eds.) *African Wildlife and Livelihoods: the promise and performance of community conservation.* James Currey. Oxford.

Arntzen, J. (2003). *An Economic View on Wildlife Management Areas in Botswana. Gaborone: IUCN/SNV CBNRM Support Programme.* CBNRM Support Programme Occasional Paper. No. 10.

Arntzen, J. W, Molokomme, D.L., Terry, E. M., Moleele, N., Tshosa, O. and Mazambani, D. (2003). 'Final Report of the Review of Community-Based Natural Resource Management in Botswana'. National CBNRM Forum. Gaborone, Botswana.

Arntzen, J. (2006). *Case study of the CBNRM programme in Botswana. Case studies on successful Southern African NRM initiatives and their impacts on poverty and governance.* USAID Frame Project. IUCN. South Africa. Pretoria.

Athawale, R.N. (2003). *Water Harvesting and Sustainable Supply in India.* Centre for Environment Education. Ahmedabad Rawat Publications. New Delhi.

Bandyopadhyay, S., Shyamsundar, P., Wang, L. and Humavindu, M.N. (2004). *Do households gain from community-based natural resource management? An evaluation of community conservancies in Namibia.* DEA Research Discussion Paper; No. 68. Directorate of Environmental Affairs. Windhoek, Namibia.

Barrow, E. and Murphree, M. (2001). 'Community conservation: from concept to practice' in Hulme, D. and Murphree, M. (eds.) *African Wildlife and Livelihoods: the promise and performance of community conservation.* James Currey. Oxford.

Barret, C. B. and Arcese, P. (1995). 'Are Integrated Conservation-development Projects (ICDPs) Sustainable? On the Conservation of Large Mammals in Sub-Saharan Africa'. *World Development.* Vol. 23. No. 7: 1073-1084.

Biggs, R. Bohensky, E., Desanker P.V., Fabricius, C., Lynam, T., Misselhorn, A.A., Musvoto, C., Mutale, M., reyers, B., Scholes, R.J., Shinkongo S., and A.S. van Jaarsveld (2004). *Nature Supporting People. The Southern Africa Millennium Ecosystem Assessment.* CSIR, Pretoria.

Bond, I. (2001). 'CAMPFIRE and the Incentives for Institutional Change' pp 227–243 in Hulme, D. and Murphree, M. (eds.) *African Wildlife and Livelihoods: the promise and performance of community conservation.* James Currey. Oxford.

Bond, I., Child, B., de la Harpe, D., Jones, B., Barnes, J., and Anderson, H. (2004). 'Private Land Contribution to Conservation in Southern Africa' in Child, B. (ed.) *Parks in Transition: Biodiversity, rural development and the bottom line.* Earthscan/IUCN South Africa. London.

Borrini-Feyuerabend, G., Pimbert, M., Farvar, M.T., Kothari, A., and Y. Renard (2004). *Sharing Power. Learning by doing in Co-management of natural resources through out the world.* IIED, London, U.K.

Brandon, K., Redford, K.H. and Sanderson S.E. (1998). *Parks in peril: people, politics and protected areas.* Island Press. Washington, DC

Brockington, D. and Igoe, J. (in press). *Anthropology, Conservation, Protected Areas and Identity Politics.*

Bromley, D. W. and Cernea, M. M. (1989). *The management of common property natural resources: some conceptual and operational fallacies.* World Bank Discussion Papers 57. World Bank. Washington D. C., USA.

Campbell, B. M., Jeffrey, S., Kozanayi, W. Luckert, M., Mutamba, M. and Zindi, C. (2002). *Household Livelihoods in Semi-Arid Regions: Options and constraints.* CIFOR. Bogor, Indonesia.

Child, B. (1988). *The role of wildlife utilisation in the sustainable development of semi-arid rangelands in Zimbabwe.* D. Phil. Thesis. Worcester College, Oxford University. Oxford, UK.

Child, B. (2004a). 'Introduction' in B. Child (ed) *Parks in Transition, Biodiversity, Rural Development and the Bottom Line.* Earthscan. London.

Child, B. (2004b). 'The Luangwa Integrated Rural Development Project, Zambia' in Fabricius, C., Koch, E., with Magome, H. and Turner, S. (eds.) *Rights, Resources and Rural Development: Community-based Natural Resource Management in Southern Africa.* Earthscan. London, UK.

Child, B., Jones, B., Mazambani, D., Mlalazi, A. and Moinuddin, H. (2003). 'Final Evaluation Report: Zimbabwe Natural Resources Management Program - USAID/Zimbabwe Strategic Objective No. 1. CAMPFIRE, Communal Areas Management Programme for Indigenous Resources'. USAID. Harare.

CIDA Forestry Advisors Network. (2004). 'Forestry profiles: Forestry, trees, and climate change: Recent experiences in Asia'. Downloaded May 2006 from: http://www.rcfa-cfan.org/english/profile.19.htm

Colchester, M. (1994). *Salvaging nature: indigenous peoples, protected areas and biodiversity conservation*. Discussion Paper No. 55. UNRISD, Geneva.

CFI (undated). 'Participatory approaches to forest carbon projects. Phase I: Methods development'. Downloaded May 2006 from: http://www.communityforestryinterna tional.org/programs/south_asia/madhya_pradesh/participatory_approaches_to_for est_carbon_projects_mp.htm

Cronkleton, M. C. (2005). 'Self-systematization of Central American experiences with bio diversity conservation and management'. Downloaded May 2006 from: http://www.cgiar.org/pdf/acicafoc_english_final.pdf

Cumming, D. H. M. and Lynam, T. J. P. (1997). *Land use changes, Wildlife Conservation and Utilisation, and the Sustainability of Agro-ecosystems in the Zambezi Valley, Final Technical Report Volume 1.*WWF. Harare, Zimbabwe.

Cumming, D. H. M. (2004). 'Performance of Parks in a Century of Change' in B. Child (ed) *Parks in Transition, Biodiversity, Rural Development and the Bottom Line*. Earthscan. London.

Desanker, P.V. and Magadza, C. (2001). Chapter 10 of the *IPCC Working Group II, Third Assessment Report.* Cambridge University Press. Cambridge, UK.

Deutsch, C. (2002). *Love & A Bag of Cement: Desertification, NGOs, and Capacity Building in Communal Lands of Southern Namibia*. Unpublished research thesis.

du Toit, R. (1999). 'Savé Valley Conservancy as a Model for the Conservation of Biodiversity in the African Semi-Arid Savanna'. Presented at the IFC-SMA Programme Conference, May 1999, Washington.

Dunham, K. M., Davies, C. and Muhwandagara, K. (2003). *Area and Quality of Wildlife Habitat in selected CAMPFIRE Districts, A Report prepared for WWF-SARPO, January.* WWF. Harare, Zimbabwe.

Durbin, J., Jones, B. T. B. and Murphree, M. W. (1997). *Namibian Community-Based Natural Resource Management Programme*. (WWF NA 0004: Namibia). Project Evaluation. WWF. Gland, Switzerland.

Ferrari, M. F. and de Vera, D. (2003). 'A "participatory" or a "rights-based" approach? Which is best for protected areas and indigenous peoples in the Philippines?' *Policy Matters 12:* 166-170.

Ferraro, P. J. and Pattanayak, S. K. (2006). 'Money for nothing? A call for empirical evaluation of biodiversity conservation investments'. *Public Library of Science Biology.* April 2006. Volume 4. Issue 4.

Fabricius, C., Koch, E., with Magome, H. and Turner, S. (eds.) (2004) *Rights, Resources and Rural Development: Community-based Natural Resource Management in Southern Africa*. Earthscan. London, UK.

Foundation for Ecological Security. (2003). *A Biodiversity Log and Strategy Input Document for the Gori River Basin, Western Himalayan Ecoregion, Uttaranchal. A sub state process under the National Biodiversity Strategy and Action Plan Indi* Munsiari, India.

63

Gommes, R. and Petrassi, F. (1996). *Rainfall Variability and Drought in Sub-Saharan Africa since 1960*. FAO Agrometeorology Series Working Paper No. 9. FAO Research, Extension and Training Division.

Grieg-Gran, M. and Bishop, J. (2004). 'How can Markets for Ecosystem Services Benefit the Poor?' in Roe, D (ed). *The Millennium Development Goals and Conservation – Managing Nature's Wealth for Society's Health*. IIED. London, UK.

Gutierrez, I., Ortiz, N. and Imbach, A. (2000) *Community Wildlife. Management in Central America: A Regional Review*. IIED Evaluating Eden Discussion Paper No. 12.

Hardin, G. (1968). 'The Tragedy of the Commons'. *Science*. 162 (1968): 1243-1248.

Hazelwood, P., Kulshrestha, G., and C. McNeil (2004) 'Linking Biodiversity Conservation and Poverty Reduction to Achieve the Millennium Development Goals.' in Roe, D. (ed.) *The Millennium Development Goals and Conservation: Managing Nature's Wealth for Society's Health*. IIED. London, UK.

Hutton, J., Adams, W. M. and Murombedzi, J. C. (2005). 'Back to the barriers?: Changing narratives in biodiversity conservation'. *Forum for Development Studies* 32, 2: 341-370.

Hulme, D. and M. Murphree (2001) 'Community Conservation as Policy. Promise and Performance.' pp 280 – 297. in Hulme, D. and Murphree, M. (eds.) *African Wildlife and Livelihoods: the promise and performance of community conservation. James Currey. Oxford*.

IPCC. (2001). *The Third Assessment of the Inter-governmental panel on climate change (IPCC)*. Cambridge University Press. Cambridge, UK.

IUCN, UNEP and WWF. (1980). *The World Conservation Strategy*. IUCN. Gland, Switzerland.

Jones, B. (2001).The Evolution of a Community-based Approach to Wildlife Management at Kunene, Namibia' in Hulme, D. and Murphree, M. (eds.) *African Wildlife and Livelihoods: the promise and performance of community conservation*. James Currey. Oxford.

Jones, B. T. B. (2004a). *Synthesis of the current status of CBNRM Policy and Legislation in Botswana, Malawi, Mozambique, Namibia, Zambia and Zimbabwe*. WWF-SARPO. Harare, Zimbabwe.

Jones, B. T. B. (2004b). *CBNRM, poverty reduction and sustainable livelihoods: Developing criteria for evaluating the contribution of CBNRM to poverty reduction and alleviation in Southern Africa*. Commons Southern Africa Occasional Paper No. 7. Centre for Applied Social Sciences, University of Zimbabwe, Harare and the Programme for Land and Agrarian Studies, University of the Western Cape, Cape Town, South Africa.

Jones, B. T. B. (2004c). *A Strategic Policy Review of Key Issues Currently Pertinent to the Implementation of CBNRM, the CBD and the UNCCD in Namibia*. Report for the Namibia Nature Foundation project 'Conservation and Development Opportunities from the Sustainable Use of Biological Diversity in the Communal Lands of Southern Africa'. Namibia Nature Foundation. Windhoek, Namibia.

Jones, B. T. B. and M. W. Murphree. (2001). 'The Evolution of Policy on Community Conservation in Namibia and Zimbabwe' in Hulme, D. and Murphree, M. (eds.) *African Wildlife and Livelihoods: the promise and performance of community conservation*. James Currey. Oxford.

Jones, B. T. B. and M. W. Murphree. (2004). 'Community-based Natural Resource Management as a Conservation Mechanism: Lessons and Directions' in Child, B. (ed.) *Parks in Transition: Biodiversity, rural development and the bottom line*. Earthscan and IUCN South Africa. London, UK.

Key to Costa Rica. (2003). 'The new key to Costa Rica, 17th edition'. Downloaded May 2006 from: http://www.keytocostarica.com/Mesoamerican-biological-corridor.htm

Kothari, A., Pathak, N., and Vania, F. (2000). *Where Communities Care: Community Based Wildlife and Ecosystem Management in South Asia*. Kalpavriksh and IIED. Delhi/Pune, India and London, UK.

Koziell, I. and McNeill, C. I. (2002). *Building on Hidden Opportunities to Achieve the Millennium Development Goals: Poverty Reduction through Conservation and Sustainable Use of Biodiversity*. IIED Opinion Series, London, UK.

Kulhari, O.P. (2003). *Arvari Catchment Biodiversity Strategy and Action Plan*. Substate site for the National Biodiversity Strategy and Action Plan, India. Tarun Bharat Sangh, India.

Leach, M., Mearns, R. and Scoones, I. (1999). 'Environmental Entitlements: Dynamics and Institutions in Community-Based Natural Resource Management'. *World Development* 27(2):225-247.

LIFE. (2004). *End of Project Report Phase II: For the period August 12, 1999 – September 30, 2004*. Windhoek: WWF-LIFE Project.

Long, S. A. (2004). 'Livelihoods in the Conservancy Study Areas' in Long, S. A. (ed.) *Livelihoods and CBNRM in Namibia: The Findings of the WILD Project. Final Technical Report of the Wildlife Integration for Livelihood Diversification Project*. Ministry of Environment and Tourism. Windhoek, Namibia.

MA. (2005a). *Living Beyond our Means: Natural Assets and Human Well-being - Statement from the Board*. Island Press. Washington DC., USA.

MA. (2005b). *Ecosystems and Human Well-being: Biodiversity synthesis*. Island Press. Washington DC., USA.

MA. (2005c). *Ecosystems and Human Well-being: General Synthesis*. Island Press. Washington DC., USA.

Magome, H. and Fabricius, C. (2004). 'Reconciling biodiversity conservation with rural development: The holy Grail of CBNRM?' in Fabricius, C., Koch, E., with Magome, H. and Turner, S. (eds.) *Rights, Resources and Rural Development: Community-based Natural Resource Management in Southern Africa. Earthscan*. London, UK.

Malhotra, K. C., Chakravarty, K. K., Bhanu, B. V., Chatterjee S., Deb, D., Gokhale Y. and Srivastava S. (2000). *Sacred Groves of India: A Travelling Exhibition*. Indira Gandhi Rashtriya Manav Sangrahalaya. Bhopal, India.

65

Mapedza, E. and Bond, I. (Submitted). 'Political Deadlocks and Devolved Wildlife Management in Zimbabwe: The Case of Nenyunga Ward'. *Journal of Environment and Development*. University of California. USA.

Murphree, M. W. (2000). 'Community-based Conservation: Old Ways, New Myths And Enduring Challenges'. Paper presented at the *Conference on African Wildlife Management in the New Millenium*. College of African Wildlife Management. Mweka, Tanzania, 13-15 December 2000.

Murphy, C., and Roe, D. (2004). 'Livelihoods and Tourism in Communal Area Conservancies' in Long, S. A. (ed.) *Livelihoods and CBNRM in Namibia: The Findings of the WILD Project. Final Technical Report of the Wildlife Integration for Livelihood Diversification Project*. Ministry of Environment and Tourism. Windhoek, Namibia.

NACSO. (2004). *Namibia's communal conservancies: A review of progress and challenges*. Namibian Association of CBNRM Support Organisations. Windhoek.

Nhantumbo, I., Chonguica, E., Anstey, S. (in preparation) *Community based natural resource management in Mozambique: The challenges of sustainability.*

Nhira, C., Baker, S., Gondo, P., Mangono, J. J. and Marunda, C. (1998). *Contesting inequality in access to forests: Zimbabwe country study*. No. 5. IIED Policy that works for forests and people series. IIED. London, UK.

Norphel, C. (2001). 'Learning from Nature. Rural Water Harvesting: Trans Himalayan Region' in Agarwal, A., Narain, S. and Khurana, I. *Making Water Everybody's Business. Practice and Policy of Water Harvesting*. Centre for Science and Environment, New Delhi.

Orrego, J. (2005). *The Plan Vivo experience with carbon service provision and the potential lessons for watershed service projects*. Edinburgh Centre for Carbon Management Ltd. Edinburgh.

Ostrom E. (1990). *Governing the Commons. The Evolution of Institutions for Collective Action*. Cambridge University Press. Cambridge, UK.

Pathak, N., Bhatt, S. and Balasinorwala, T. (2004). *Community Conserved Areas: A Bold Frontier for Conservation*. Briefing Note 5. TILCEPA, CEESP-WCPA (IUCN), CMWG, CENESTA. Iran.

Pathak N., Kothari A., and Roe D. (2005). 'Conservation with social justice? The role of community conserved areas in achieving the Millennium Development Goals' in Bigg, T. and Satterthwaite, D. (eds.) *How to Make Poverty History: The central role of local organizations in meeting the MDGs*. IIED. London, UK.

Pearce, D. (2005) *Investing in Environmental Wealth for Poverty Reduction*. Prepared on behalf of the Poverty Environment Partnership, UNDP, New York.

Pisupati, B and Warner, E. (2003). *Biodiversity and the Millennium Development Goals*. IUCN Regional Biodiversity Programme, Asia.

Reid, H. (2004). 'Climate change and biodiversity impacts' in Roe, D. (ed.) *The Millennium Development Goals and Conservation - Managing Nature's Wealth for Society's Health*. IIED. London, UK.

Local action, global aspirations

Roe D. *et al.* (2000) *Evaluating Eden: Exploring the Myths and Realities of Community Wildlife Management.* IIED, London.

Roe, D. (2003) 'The Millennium Development Goals and natural resources management: reconciling sustainable livelihoods and resource conservation or fuelling a divide?' in Satterthwaite, D. (ed). *The MDGs and Local Processes: Hitting the Target or Missing the Point?* IIED, London.

Rozemeijer, N. (2003). 'CBNRM in Botswana' in *Parks in Transition: Conservation, Development and the Bottom Line, Vol. II.* IUCN Southern African Sustainable Use Specialist Group. Lusaka, Zambia.

RUPFOR. (2002). *Joint Forest Management: A Decade of Partnership. Joint Forest Management Cell.* Resource Unit for Participatory Forestry, Ministry of Environment and Forests, Government of India. New Delhi, India.

Sachs, J. (2005). *The End of Poverty: Economic Possibilities for Our Time.* Penguin Press. London. U.K.

SADC. (2003). *The Regional Indicative Strategic Development Plan. Southern African Development Community.* Gaborone, Botswana.

Saterson, K., Margoluis, R. and Salafsky, N. (eds.) (1998). *Measuring Conservation Impact: An Interdisciplinary Approach to Project Monitoring and Evaluation.* Proceedings from a BSP symposium at the Society for Conservation Biology Annual Meeting. Biodiversity Support Program. Washington, DC.

Shackleton, S, and Shackleton C. (2004). 'Everyday resources are valuable enough for community-based natural resource management programme support: Evidence from South Africa' in: Fabricius, C., Koch, E., with Magome, H. and Turner, S. (eds.) *Rights, Resources and Rural Development: Community-based Natural Resource Management in Southern Africa.* Earthscan. London, UK.

Sibanda, B. (2004). 'Community Wildlife Management in Zimbabwe: The case of CAMPFIRE in the Zambezi Valley' in: Fabricius, C., Koch, E., with Magome, H. and Turner, S. (eds.) *Rights, Resources and Rural Development: Community-based Natural Resource Management in Southern Africa.* Earthscan. London, UK.

SICAP. (2003). 'The Central American Protected Areas System: A key arena for conserving biological diversity'. Downloaded May 2006 from: http://www.ccad.ws/documentos/comitestecnicos/informeSICAP2003english.pdf

Taylor, R. (2006). 'Case study: CAMPFIRE, Zimbabwe' in *Case studies on successful Southern African NRM initiatives and their impacts on poverty and governance. USAID Frame Project.* IUCN South Africa. Pretoria, South Africa.

Terborgh, J. (1999). *Requiem for Nature.* Island Press. Washington, DC.

TPCG, Kalpavriksh. (2005). *Securing India's Future: Final Technical Report of the National Biodiversity Strategy and Action Plan.* NBSAP Technical and Policy Core Group. Delhi, Kalpavriksh, Pune.

67

Turner, R. (2004). 'Communities, conservation, and tourism-based development: Can community-based nature tourism live up to its promise?' Paper presented at the 'Breslauer Symposium on Natural Resources in Africa' held at the University of California, Berkeley, March 2004.

Turner, S. (2004). 'Community-based natural resource management and rural livelihoods' in Fabricius, C., Koch, E., with Magome, H. and Turner, S. (eds.) *Rights, Resources and Rural Development: Community-based Natural Resource Management in Southern Africa. Earthscan.* London, UK.

UN. (1992) *Agenda 21: The United Nations Programme of Action From Rio,* United Nations, New York, NY.

UNCBD. 'Decision V/6. Ecosystem approach'. Downloaded May 2006 from: http://www.biodiv.org/decisions/default.aspx?m=COP-05&id=7148&lg=0

UN. (2000). 'The UN Millennium Development Goals'. Downloaded June 2006 from: http://www.un.org/millenniumgoals/goals.html

UNEP. (2000) *Global Environment Outlook.* United Nations Environment Programme, Nairobi.

UNFCCC. (undated). 'The Rio Conventions: Climate change, biodiversity, and desertification'. Downloaded May 2006 from: http://unfccc.int/essential_back ground/feeling_the_heat/items/2916.php

Vaughan, C., Long, S.A., Katjiua, J., Mulonga, S., and Murphy, C. (2004). 'Wildlife use and livelihoods' in Long, S. A. (ed.) *Livelihoods and CBNRM in Namibia: The Findings of the WILD Project. Final Technical Report of the Wildlife Integration for Livelihood Diversification Project.* Ministry of Environment and Tourism. Windhoek, Namibia.

Western, D. and Wright, M. A. (eds.) (1994). Natural Connections: *Perspectives in community-based conservation.* Island Press. Washington DC, USA.

Weaver, L. C and Skyer, P. (2003). 'Conservancies: Integrating wildlife land-use options into the livelihood, development and conservation strategies of Namibian communities'. Paper presented at the Vth World Parks Congress of IUCN to the Animal Health and Development (AHEAD) Forum, Durban, September 8-17.

WCED. (1987). *Our Common Future.* Oxford University Press. Oxford, UK.

WRI. (2005) *The Wealth of the Poor. Managing Ecosystems to Fight Poverty.* World Resources Institute. Washington DC.

WRI. (2006). 'Carbon sequestration projects'. Downloaded May 2006 from: http://climate.wri.org/sequestration.cfm

World Bank. (1986). *The World Bank's Operational Policy on Wildlands: Their Protection and Management in Economic Development.* The World Bank. Washington, D.C.

World Bank. (2001). *World Development Report 200/2001: Attacking Poverty.* Oxford University Press. New York.

World Bank. (2000). *Community Driven Development in Africa.* www.worldbank.org/cdd.

World Bank. (2005). *Where is the Wealth of Nations?* Washington DC.